THE HIDDEN CHILDREN

THE HIDDEN CHILDREN

by

HOWARD GREENFELD

HOUGHTON MIFFLIN COMPANY
Boston

For information about this and other Houghton Mifflin trade and reference books and multimedia products, visit The Bookstore at Houghton Mifflin on the World Wide Web at http://www.hmco.com/trade/.

Manufactured in the United States of America

Book design by Amy Hill

The text of this book is set in Transitional 521.

VB 10 9 8 7 6 5 4

Library of Congress Cataloging-in-Publication Data
Greenfeld, Howard.
The hidden children / by Howard Greenfeld.
    p. cm.
    Summary: Describes the experiences of those Jewish children who were forced to go into hiding during the Holocaust and survived to tell about it.
    RNF ISBN 0-395-66074-2 PAP ISBN 0-395-86138-1
    1. Holocaust, Jewish (1939–1945)—Personal narratives—Juvenile literature. 2. Jewish children—Biography—Juvenile literature. 3. Holocaust survivors—Biography—Juvenile literature. 4. World War, 1939–1945—Children—Juvenile literature. [1. Holocaust, Jewish (1939–1945) 2. Holocaust survivors. 3. Jews—Europe.] I. Title.
D804.3.G72 1993
940.53'18'0922—dc20   93-20325
[B]   CIP AC

For My Parents

Evelyn Greenfeld   *(1899–1993)*

and

Isadore Greenfeld   *(1893–1976)*

With Love

CONTENTS

ACKNOWLEDGMENTS

I could never have written this book without the support and encouragement of my editor and publisher, Norma Jean Sawicki; nor could I have written it without the help of Ann Shore, a remarkable woman—an accomplished painter who, herself a hidden child, has selflessly devoted most of her seemingly boundless energy and intelligence to her duties as president of the Hidden Child Foundation. I am most grateful to both of them.

I am especially grateful to the hidden children who agreed to share their memories with me and to let me use their photos in this book. Some of them prefer to remain anonymous, and I honor their request. The others include the following: Maya Freed, Jack Goldstein, Rachelle Goldstein, Rosette Goldstein, Fran Greene, Roald Hoffmann, Benno Horowitz, Edith Knoll, Klemak Nowicki, Zelda Polofsky, Stefanie Seltzer, Frank Siegel, Alice Sondike, Gisele Warshawsky, and Eva Wollenberger.

INTRODUCTION

According to the dictionary, the word *holocaust* means destruction, devastation, total consummation by fire. Today, the word refers specifically to what is surely one of the darkest periods in history, the years of terror during which one nation and its leader—Nazi Germany and Adolf Hitler—tried by all possible means to annihilate the Jews of Europe, and succeeded in destroying six million of them.

It was a unique, unprecedented period. The Jews were to be killed not because they held territory Hitler wanted nor because of power they possessed nor because of any idea they held. According to the Nazis, the Jews were a diseased race, and Hitler would not be satisfied until every European Jew—man, woman, and child—had been destroyed.

During Hitler's reign of power, there were many others who suffered from the dictator's wrath. There were the innocent victims

1

of all wars—the soldiers who followed orders blindly and were killed during battle, and the civilians who died as a result of the bombings of their cities and villages and homes. There were also millions of courageous non-Jews, members of resistance groups who actively opposed Nazism in Germany and in the countries the Nazis conquered, who were put to death. Furthermore, at least a quarter of a million Gypsies, thousands of homosexuals, men and women who were physically handicapped, and those classified as "mentally defective"—none of them guilty of any crime—were killed because, by Hitler's definition, they were "impure" and not members of the "master race."

This book is not about these victims. It deals with one specific group, the Jewish children who survived the Holocaust by going into hiding.

The statistics are astonishing. Only 11 percent of the approximately 1.7 million European Jews under the age of sixteen alive in 1939 survived the Second World War. In other words, 1.5 million young Jews were killed during the Holocaust. Of these, the most famous is Anne Frank, who, together with her family, hid from the Nazis in an attic in Amsterdam until she was caught and sent to a concentration camp where she died. She was but one of many children who died in death camps, and her story is well known because of the extraordinarily moving diary she kept while in hiding. But there were thousands of other Jewish children—somewhere between ten thousand and one hundred thousand of them—who were hidden during the Holocaust, who were not caught and who survived.

The hidden children I interviewed for this book are now in their fifties and sixties and well established in the United States. Most of them found it difficult to speak of the past. Our conversations were always painful and disturbing; they were always moving.

Each man and woman has his or her own tale to tell, but a common thread runs through them all. Though all European children—non-Jewish as well as Jewish—suffered during the Second World War, these Jewish children were not allowed to go to school, they couldn't maintain friendships, and they were usually deprived of one or both parents. They were hunted and threatened with death, and in order to live, they had to go into hiding.

Some of these children remained "visible." Masking their identities with Christian names and fictitious stories of their past and their origins, they hid their Jewishness, at great emotional cost. This task demanded enormous ingenuity and never-ending vigilance. The majority of the hidden children, however, were forced to disappear from sight. Taken from their homes and towns, they were separated from their friends and families. Most were either given refuge in convents and orphanages or adopted and protected by courageous non-Jewish families. Some experienced inhuman suffering, living for long periods of time in haylofts, cramped attics, or airless basements. A few endured abuse at the hands of their rescuers. All of them learned to lie, to deny their true identities, to conceal their emotions, and to remain silent in potentially dangerous situations.

The people I interviewed are remarkable; they are what we might call high achievers. Among them are several educators, two psychologists, a dentist, a civil engineer, and a scientist who has won the Nobel prize in chemistry. Most were born to middle- or upper-class families that placed a high value on the education of their children. Many families were deeply religious and regularly observed Jewish customs. Others, less religious, were made aware of their Jewishness only by their persecutors, who defined them as Jews. A large number of the people with whom I spoke were hidden in Poland or Belgium. This may be pure coincidence, although we know that there were more Jews in Poland than in any other European country and the Belgians were especially hospitable to Jews and adept at hiding them.

Today, these men and women are articulate and sensitive, feeling a responsibility to make their stories known to their children and grandchildren so that the tragic mistakes of the past will not be repeated. They firmly believe that the smallest sign of injustice, of racism, must be vigorously opposed before it has a chance to grow.

The men and women who granted me these interviews are adults remembering events and experiences that took place many years ago, in circumstances they would prefer to forget. Although they are uncommonly perceptive as a group, their memories of details are not always precise or correct. It seems to me unimportant that there may be some inconsistencies in dates, or that the names of towns and villages and their exact locations may sometimes be mistaken or unknown. What matters is the substance of these moving, deeply felt accounts of their childhoods.

I read stories about animals in the forest that were being protected. There were laws that you can't shoot a deer, and all of a sudden it dawned on me that these animals were better off than we were. You couldn't hunt them, while we had absolutely no protection. What really bothered me the most, I think, was there was no safety net. There was no one you could go to. You couldn't go to the police, you couldn't go anywhere. It was like being worse than an animal. I realized at the time that our level of existence was worse than an animal. They had some protection, there were only certain months you could shoot them. . . .

—Jack Goldstein

PART ONE

THE BEGINNINGS

ONE

The seeds of anti-Semitism were planted many centuries before Adolf Hitler was born. From the beginning of Christianity, the myth that the Jews were responsible for Christ's death persisted, and Jews were denounced as Christ killers. In the Middle Ages, the Jews were accused of causing the plague that killed millions of Europeans, and for centuries they were accused of killing Christian children so that the blood of these children could be used for religious purposes—in the baking of matzo for the Jewish festival of Passover, for example. For centuries, too, they have been depicted on stage and in caricatures as satanic, inhuman creatures.

From time to time, in different parts of Europe, Jews were excluded from certain professions; prevented from owning land; forced to wear special articles of clothing so that they might be easily identified as Jews; deprived of their property; and made to live in ghettos, separated from the non-Jewish population. They often served as a scapegoat, blamed when a country suffered economically or in war, and at different times they were expelled—from Spain, France, England, and Portugal, among other countries.

Periodically, they were banished from Germany. As far back as the twelfth century, thousands of Jews were massacred in what is now Germany, and, in later times, without provocation, Jewish homes throughout the region were destroyed, Jewish cemeteries desecrated, and synagogues burned to the ground. In the nineteenth century, German hatred of the Jews intensified, and in the 1870s a journalist named Wilhelm Marr introduced the term *anti-Semitism*, defining Jews as a "slave" race, incapable of salvation by conversion as had been believed in the past, and therefore inherently different from other human beings. By the end of the century, anti-Semitic politicians had entered the government, and anti-Semitic books and pamphlets were published and gained wide acceptance and popularity.

It was not until the 1930s, however, that Hitler made anti-Semitism the official government policy in Germany. Following World War I, the climate for the rise of such a disaster was favorable. Germany had lost the war and had been humiliated; this once-proud, strong nation was reduced to the status of a second-rate power. It was severely punished by the victorious Allies. Under the Treaty of Versailles, which officially concluded the war in 1919, Germany was forced to give up land, drastically reduce the size of its armed forces, and to pay billions of dollars to the victors to compensate for the suffering the war had caused. As a result, the German economy collapsed during the early 1920s.

Crippling inflation made the German currency practically worthless. Unemployment followed, and, with it, hardships and despair.

During this period of discontent, the Nazi party, led by Hitler, was founded. Born in 1889, Hitler had served in the army during the First World War, after which, in 1920, he entered politics and helped to found the new party. Obsessed with dreams of glory for the superior "pure" German race and with a profound hatred of the Jews, whom he blamed for all of his country's problems, he was a fiery speaker. He had an uncanny ability to rouse a crowd to anger, and his message clearly responded to a need in the German people to regain their self-esteem.

At first, his appeal was limited. In 1928, when Germany began to recover economically and signs of prosperity appeared, his party gained only 12 of 489 seats in the country's parliamentary election. Soon afterward, however, following the onset of the Great Depression in the United States in 1929, the German economy again collapsed. Millions of Germans were out of work, and the country desperately looked for a strong leader, one not connected with established parties.

Hitler was such a man. A brilliant politician, he skillfully played on the public's dreams of renewed glory and its hatred of the Jews. His rise to power was rapid. In September 1930, the Nazis became the second largest political party in Germany, and in the elections of July 1932, they gained more seats in parliament than did any other party. Though his was still not a majority party, following this election Hitler was offered the position of vice-chancellor by Germany's president, Paul von Hindenburg. Not satisfied, Hitler demanded to be named chancellor (prime minister). Von Hindenburg refused, but after a second inconclusive election held in November, he acquiesced, and in January 1933, Hitler was named chancellor of Germany.

Though legally appointed to his position, Hitler soon established an absolute dictatorship. Only a month after his appointment, he suspended all civil liberties, including freedom of the press, and in April he sanctioned a national boycott of all Jewish businesses. In July, the Nazi party was declared Germany's only political party.

With good reason, many of Germany's half million Jews (about 1 percent of the population) started to leave their country following Hitler's assumption of power, emigrating to Palestine (now the State of Israel), Western Europe, Great Britain, and the United States. Many others, however, remained blindly optimistic even after anti-Semitic laws were put into effect in 1935, robbing Jews of all their remaining rights. These Jews believed that Hitler would fall and the "true" Germany would somehow be restored. By November 1938, only 150,000 Jews had left Germany.

It wasn't long, however, before the remaining 350,000 German Jews understood that their situation was hopeless. The turning point came on the night of November 9, 1938, a night that will always be remembered as *Kristallnacht,* or the Night of the Broken Glass. Using as an excuse the shooting of an official in the German Embassy in Paris by a young German Jewish student who had been outraged by news of German atrocities toward his people, the Nazis launched a series of vicious attacks on the Jewish population. It was a night of unprecedented horror throughout the entire country. Jewish homes and shops were broken into, looted, and destroyed. Synagogues had their windows smashed with hammers and axes, and many were burned to the ground.

Jews were chased down the streets and beaten or shot, and their holy books were burned on makeshift bonfires. Twenty-four hours later, an estimated ninety-one Jews had been killed and more than thirty thousand had been arrested.

In the days following *Kristallnacht*, the Jews were forced to pay the government for damages done to their own property, and all insurance monies due them was confiscated by the state. Furthermore, it was decreed that all Jewish property, including art and jewelry, and all Jewish-owned businesses would be transferred to non-Jews.

Excluded from German economic life, even those Jews who had at first been reluctant to leave their country understood the need to emigrate as soon as possible. But it was too late for most. Money needed to make the move was increasingly difficult to raise, and transportation was severely limited. Most important, few countries were willing to accept large numbers of Jewish refugees; quotas were limited and visas were difficult to obtain. As a result, only another 150,000 Jews were able to leave.

It soon became clear that Hitler's plans to annihilate the Jews extended beyond Germany's borders. His goal was to conquer the entire continent of Europe. In March 1938, his army had entered neighboring Austria and declared it a part of the German Reich. Anti-Jewish laws were immediately put into effect. One year later, Hitler invaded and occupied Czechoslovakia, and on September 1, 1939, he sent his troops into Poland. Two days later, France and Great Britain responded by declaring war on Germany. It was the beginning of the Second World War.

Neither France nor Britain was prepared to stop the German advance, and on September 27, 1939, Poland surrendered. The country's three million Jews—the largest Jewish population in Europe—were immediately subjected to Hitler's racial policies.

The plight of the Jews seemed hopeless as Germany threatened to swallow up the entire continent. In April 1940, German troops invaded and quickly conquered Denmark and Norway. The following month, Holland and Belgium, both of which had taken in many Jewish refugees from Germany and Poland after the rise of Hitler, collapsed before the German army, as would France shortly afterward.

The Jews were trapped; very few avenues of escape remained. A few thousand headed toward the south of France, traveling on crowded roads, subject to constant strafing by German planes. Some managed to cross the Pyrenees and reach neutral Spain and Portugal. Others found refuge in Switzerland. For most, however, the only hope lay in crossing the North Sea and seeking asylum in England.

It was a time of terror and chaos. Thousands of refugees left the cities and jammed the highways in a desperate effort to reach the coast. There was a steady procession of cars, wagons, and wheelbarrows, filled with frightened people hoping, without any real plan, to reach safety.

Gisele Warshawsky, today an administrator at Queens College in New York, and her family were among them. Born in Leipzig, Germany, in 1934, Gisele was the third child of Moses and Rosa Soldinger, successful linen merchants, who had been born in Poland. Her brother and sister were many years older than she, and because their parents were often away from home, young Gisele was often left in their care. Too young to be aware of the threat of Nazism, she remembers her first years as happy and carefree. Theirs was a warm and loving household, and she took great pleasure in the Jewish customs—the holidays, the Friday night dinners, and the lighting of the candles—that they faithfully observed.

In 1938, however, everything changed. Without warning, the family was awakened in the middle of the night by the police and taken to the railroad station. There, along with hundreds of other Jews, they were told that they were to be deported to Poland. The Germans wanted to rid their country of all "foreign" Jews. The German police kept careful records of the Jewish population—each person's legal status, place of birth, and residence—but in this case the Germans were mistaken. Gisele's father was able to produce proof that he and his wife were stateless and thus no longer Polish citizens, and that their children had been born in Germany. For these reasons, they were allowed to return to their home.

Deportation to Poland, where life for Jews had become unbearable, had been avoided, but by the end of 1938, it was obvious that the family would have to leave Germany in order to survive. Their first choice was the United States, but visas were difficult to obtain and the trip would be costly, so they were forced to settle for their second choice, neighboring Belgium, which, they felt, they could easily reach by illegal means.

It was decided that Moses would be the first to attempt an escape, but at the border he was captured by the Belgians and taken to prison. After two weeks, the family received word that he had taken ill with pneumonia and been moved to a hospital in Antwerp. Because of the gravity of the illness, his wife was given permission to enter Belgium, where she arrived three days before his death, in March 1939.

That May, Gisele and her sister—her brother had preceded

them in order to arrange for their father's funeral—arrived in Antwerp. They had been led out of Germany by a Belgian Gentile woman who had been hired by their mother to obtain false papers for them and escort them personally on the train ride to Antwerp, posing as their mother. The family, reunited but fatherless, was able to begin what they hoped would be a normal life in the Belgian city.

Such a life was becoming impossible for the Jews, however. Only a year later, after the conquest of Belgium, the Soldinger family moved again, joining hordes of Jews who frantically packed their belongings, fled the cities, and took to the roads in an effort to reach England.

Gisele Soldinger Warshawsky at age five in 1939.

My family packed up and began marching, along with other refugees, out of the cities. We were hoping to reach any waterways, in order to board any ship leaving for England. If we heard rumors of a boat leaving from anywhere, we would make our way to that place. We would never separate, and taking so many people into very crowded ships was not possible. We heard of ships torpedoed after leaving a port and people drowning in the cold waters of the North Sea.

We encountered hardships marching over Belgium—lack of food, lack of money, unable to buy food. On we walked, sometimes through the night, not sleeping or resting. Farmers along the way gave us food at times. I must have been a resilient little girl to walk as I did, never complaining.

German bombers began strafing civilians walking on roads. This occurred several times a day. We escaped so many times by pure luck, when we threw ourselves into ditches on the road. Many were killed during these raids.

Some Jews had a more specific destination in mind. Late in May 1940, following the fall of the Belgian army, 850 boats—freighters, fishing boats, sailing vessels, anything that could move in the water—had crossed the twenty-four miles of the English Channel from England to the French port of Dunkirk, to evacuate and bring back to England more than 350,000 British and French troops that had been trapped near the French coast by the German army. It was one of the most daring and courageous rescue operations in history, and a number of the Jewish refugees felt they might be a part of it. Unfortunately, they were mistaken.

Among those who hoped to escape via this route was the family of Jack Goldstein. Jack and his twin brother, Bobby, had been brought up in Vienna, Austria. His family—Orthodox Jews, intensely aware of their Jewishness—had led a more than comfortable life; his father was in the textile business and had his own store.

On Jack's third birthday, March 13, 1938, Hitler's army had entered the Austrian capital, and the Austrian chancellor had declared his country's union with the German Reich. It was time, Jack's father realized, for the family to leave the

Jack Goldstein (right) with his brother Bruno and their father, whose briefcase is hiding the yellow star some Jews were forced to wear.

country. Many far-sighted Jews had left as early as 1933, believing that Hitler's annexation of Austria, with the subsequent persecution of the Jews, was inevitable.

In August 1938, Jack's father filed an application for entry to the United States, where his brother had gone. But there was a long waiting list, and the quota of Jews allowed to emigrate to America was small, so the Goldsteins decided to go first to Belgium, where entry procedures were far simpler. They settled there sometime in 1939.

Jack Goldstein is now a successful civil engineer, living in Maplewood, New Jersey. His memories of life in Belgium are the vague, inexact impressions of a four-year-old child. He remembers that his father was taken away by the Belgian police in May 1940. Accused of being a German spy because of his German accent, he was sent to a number of internment camps, where he remained until August 1941, when he escaped and was reunited with his family. And Jack remembers most clearly his family's departure for Dunkirk, not long after his father's arrest.

We heard about the evacuations of the British Expeditionary Force, so most of the Jews in Brussels—I think every Jew in Brussels—said, This is our way out. We'll go to Dunkirk and they'll evacuate us to England and we'll escape this. At the time, my mother's oldest sister was also with us, and she didn't have the right papers. There was a trucker who took us, and we paid him a certain amount to take us to the coast. The whole trip is only about maybe a hundred kilometers, sixty or seventy miles. But at a certain point, the trucker became very nervous and said to my mother, Look, she [my aunt] has to go, because she can jeopardize this whole truck—

they had about thirty people on the truck. My mother said No, she stays with her sister. So, to make a long story short, the four of us started walking. We walked with our belongings. Bobby and I were five-year-olds and it was hot, we didn't have anything to drink, anything to eat, we became nudges. *My mother was a little woman, about five foot two, maybe less, and I still have guilt, we let her carry everything. I don't know how she did it.*

At night, of course, there were no hotels—we stayed in shelters. They converted churches and schools to shelters, and refugees like us stayed in them. I don't remember what my mother did to get us some bread or some water. And during the night, there was continuous bombing—you couldn't sleep at night, all night, and I remember my brother crying, he wanted to live, he didn't want to die. It was terrible.

The road was lined with dead soldiers and dead horses. It was a very bad scene. It was hot. Finally, we found out that at Dunkirk, they were not evacuating any civilians, only the British soldiers— they were the only ones. The best thing to do was to go back to our apartment in Brussels.

Rachelle Silberman and her family also returned to their home in Brussels following an attempt to escape to England. Rachelle is now Rachelle Goldstein, the wife of Jack Goldstein, and I spoke to her the same afternoon I interviewed her husband in their comfortable suburban home. The two had met at a dance in upstate New York in 1955, and in the course of a conversation they learned that their wartime experiences had been similar, that they had both been saved by the same man, and that both of their families had tried to leave continental Europe through France.

Rachelle, born in Brussels in 1939, was only nine months old at the time of the defeat of the Belgian army, so she was too young to remember the exodus. Her mother, however, told her how the family, having packed all the possessions they could carry, joined thousands of other refugees in their quest for safety:

My mother tells the story of sleeping in barns on the road to France. At one point, the Germans passed us. They were on the road with their tanks and trucks and whatnot. Some of the Germans, according to my mother, were even kind to the refugees and threw cans of food down to them. (No, not at their heads.) They actually threw cans of condensed and evaporated milk and all that, and food. My mother thought it might be poison, so she wouldn't touch it. It was some paranoia on her part at the time, I guess. Maybe not. Who knows? But once the Germans passed us, the Germans said, Go home. And so we did.

Rachelle and her family just before they took to the road in the spring of 1940.

Frank Siegel, seven years old at the time, and his family also left their home in Brussels after the fall of Belgium. Letters from relatives in Poland had warned them of the terrible fate that would await them under the German occupation, so they, too, attempted to escape via Dunkirk. They also failed. The ship that they had hoped would take them to England never arrived—they were told it had sunk—and they were turned back and ordered to return to their home. Today, Frank teaches French in a high school near New York City. He remembers joining the other refugees in the desperate, chaotic flight, and he remembers with horror an incident that occurred on their way back to Brussels. His mother, who spoke German, asked a German soldier when the war would end, and he replied without hesitation: "When we kill all the Jews, that's when the war will end."

TWO

By the end of 1940, as Hitler completed his conquest of the Continent, the Jews were trapped. Those who had tried to escape—and failed—returned to their homes to carry on as best they could.

They faced increasingly cruel and severe restrictions. They were no longer able to work where they wanted to, and they were no longer allowed to own property. Most of them lived apart from the rest of the population, publicly ostracized and identified as Jews by a yellow star that they had to wear in public. Their travel was restricted to certain hours and they had to obey strict curfews.

Jewish children were barred from schools, public playgrounds, swimming pools, and parks. Separated from their non-Jewish friends, they were suddenly, and for no reason that they could understand, made to feel ashamed of themselves. They were scorned for being "different," and often their closest friends turned against them.

As oppressive as these living conditions were for the Jews, daily life had changed dramatically for everyone. There were bombings, food was rationed, and, in most cases, a father or a brother went off to war. Death was ever-present.

It was not until the middle of 1941 that the very existence of the Jews was endangered. The turning point came in June 1941, when Germany invaded its former ally, the Soviet Union. At this time the first mass murders of Jews occurred throughout Eastern Europe. Entire Jewish communities were ruthlessly destroyed. Polish Jews, who had been forced to live in ghettos—separated from the rest of the city by barbed wire, high walls, or wooden fences—were rounded up and sent either to concentration camps, where they lived in subhuman conditions before they were put to death, or to forced labor camps, where they were worked to death.

Within a few months, a similar fate was planned for the Jews of Western Europe. On July 31, 1941, orders were given by one of Hitler's most trusted assistants, Hermann Goering, to "carry out all the necessary preparations with regard to organizational matters for bringing about a complete solution of the Jewish question in the German sphere of influence in Europe." And on January 20, 1942, thirteen leaders of the Nazi government met in a luxurious villa at Wannsee, a suburb of Berlin, to work out detailed, concrete plans for what became known as the Final Solution—the complete destruction of the Jewish population of Europe. These plans included not only the complex arrangements for the rounding up and transportation of Europe's Jews to death camps in Eastern Europe but also a thorough, scientific study of the most efficient means by which the Jews would then be killed. Ten days after this meeting, Hitler publicly announced that the result of the war would be "the complete annihilation of the Jews." The hour would come, he was certain, when "the most evil enemy of all time would be finished, at least for a thousand years."

As news of Hitler's pronouncements spread, the Jews waited in fear. It was no longer possible to live openly as Jews: they had to disappear or somehow establish false identities. Because their true identities and whereabouts were carefully recorded by local government officials, creating new identities would be a complex and difficult matter. First, however, and of the greatest importance, they had to secure as best they could the survival of their young children.

There was only one way of saving these children, and that was by hiding them. Hiding a child was considerably less complicated than was hiding an adult. Unlike adults, small children were not required to carry official documents. Furthermore, Jewish children aroused fewer suspicions because they could blend in with the large number of non-Jewish children who became orphans of war. Nonetheless, plans had to be carefully and hastily made.

In most cases, arrangements for hiding were made through personal contacts. One person knew another person who knew still another individual who was willing to give refuge to a Jewish child. Networks of potential rescuers were established. Many Christians, motivated by compassion and moral concern, were willing to risk their own lives in order to protect the lives of others. In addition to these individuals—who became known as "righteous Gentiles"—there were clandestine anti-Nazi organizations, resistance groups dedicated to the downfall of the Nazi-dominated occupying governments, whose members were willing and able to assist Jews in search of hiding places. There were also humanitarian social or religious groups formed specifically to supply these children with money and false documents and find them safe places of refuge.

The decision to send a child into hiding was a difficult one for both the parents and the children. The separation was painful, but necessary. It was far easier to hide one child than it was to hide an entire family; there was less risk of discovery. In some cases, one parent could accompany the child or children. This was almost always the mother, as most adult males had been sent to labor camps. However, most of the time these young children would be sent away alone, entrusted to strangers upon whom they would be entirely dependent.

Travel to a hiding place, usually far from home, was a terrifying experience for these children. In most cases, it involved a train ride under mysterious circumstances to an unknown destination. Unable to fully understand why they were being sent away, they knew instinctively that they were in danger.

Jack Goldstein was among those children sent into hiding. In the beginning he was relatively fortunate. He traveled with his twin brother and was accompanied by a man of extraordinary compassion and sensitivity. His family had decided to send their sons into hiding in early 1944. To help them, they made contact through a non-Jewish neighbor with the Reverend Bruno Reynders, a Belgian monk known as Père Bruno. This courageous man, who was in his early thirties at the time, risked his life daily by helping, often in cooperation with the Belgian resistance, to find hiding places for Jews threatened with deportation. At the end of the war, it was estimated that he was responsible for the salvation of almost four hundred children and some one hundred adults.

The brothers first met Père Bruno at the railroad station, just before their departure from Brussels. Their departure was made less difficult not only because of the reassuring presence of Père Bruno but also because of the novelty of the train ride. Jack remembers that ride:

The train ride stands out in my mind because we had been deprived of all such things. We came to Brussels when we were four. The war started when we were five, so we hadn't been on any trains. The train experience was a fantastic experience for us—we loved it, we loved the train. My brother and I played games, he went up into the luggage rack, we played hide and seek. . . . He [Père Bruno] let us play. He didn't say, Look, be serious—this is a serious mission, I am risking my life for you kids, so don't fool around, just sit in your corner and read something and keep quiet. He was very tolerant and he let us play.

Their first stop was somewhere up north—Jack isn't sure just where it was—at the home of a doctor. There, in the evening, Père Bruno told the boys that they would no longer be known by the Jewish name of Goldstein—their new name would be Kestemont. Their first names and their date of birth could be left the same, however. Before leaving them, he gave them false identity cards and ration booklets; food, of course, was scarce. The following morning the doctor told them he would take them by car to their final destination. This hiding place, a convent called Colonie

Saint Jean Berchmans, was situated in Maaseik, close to the border with Holland. The trip, as Jack remembers it, was harrowing:

The doctor told us, Look, we're going to pass several controls, because the Germans controlled the routes and they stopped you every ten or fifteen miles and they'd look at papers. And, of course the papers that we had were phony, and the police would examine even the doctor's papers. So he said, Look, we're going to tell them that I'm a doctor, that you're sick, and that I am taking you to a hospital. Look sick, don't say anything. Don't answer them. Just cough and look sick.

I remember that I knew that it was not a game. This was serious business. I don't know what kind of a car he had, I just remember that it was a black car. And that was exciting, too, because I can't recall having been in a car any other time in all those years. But he took us in disguise and, sure enough, the Germans stopped us. He had covered us with a blanket and then they lifted the cover to look at us, and we coughed, and they talked to us, and we didn't answer them. The doctor said we were feverish. Then he took us to the convent.

Jack and Bruno at Colonie Saint Jean Berchmans. Jack is directly in front of the second woman from the right. Bruno is in front of him.

Another youngster, Benno Horowitz, went into hiding with his parents and his younger brother, but his train ride to their hiding place was more frightening than Jack Goldstein's had been.

The Horowitz family had lived in Germany

until 1933, but when Hitler took power that year, Benno's father, understanding the threat to the Jews of Germany, decided it was time to leave. Their destination was Paris, where the family prospered. Then, in June 1940, when the Germans conquered France, they were once again uprooted. The country was divided into two parts, with the north, including Paris, under direct control of the Nazis while the southern half of the country remained in the hands of the French. Feeling threatened, the Horowitz family decided to move to the city of Lyon, in the south.

In November 1942, however, the Nazis took over the whole of France, and Benno and his family were again forced to move. This time they had to go into hiding. Benno remembers the chaos that followed the German decision to govern the entire country:

There was pandemonium among the Jews—what to do, where to go. No hope. Nowhere to go. So a lot of people started running away to Switzerland from Lyon. The Swiss were surprised, taken by surprise, and they let in maybe ten or twenty thousand, but after that, they stopped them. And they didn't just shove them back across the forest. They'd stop them and hand them to the Germans. It was their end. My father didn't want to take a chance like that. He did not want to take a chance to go to Switzerland. So we picked up our false papers and went to the French Alps.

He also remembers the harrowing journey from Lyon to the French Alps:

We made a huge mistake. The European trains are organized in compartments, eight people per compartment. We had identity cards *that were made in the same little village. The problem was that they all looked the same although we had different names. In the train, there were checks, police checks, and we were just sitting there. I was at the end of this row of four, and my father was sitting at the window at the end of that row, and the police came to check papers. They went through us. When they got to my father, they looked at his paper. It was a false card. It was written by a professional. But they didn't trust his identity. He looked—what the Germans described as Jewish-looking, he looked a little bit like that. So they put his card in their pocket and continued. Then they came to me. And they took my card. A different name. He [a policeman] took out the card of my father's and compared the two cards, and he saw that the handwritings were very similar. Because they were done in the same place. So he asked me, looking me in the face, "Do you know this man?" And my heart sank. I just didn't know what to say. So I said no. He gave me my card back. He put my father's card in his pocket. And he went out. The train continued. At the next station, they came onto the train and took my father down into the station. So we got off, too.*

Another Jewish child, Rosette Goldstein, born Rosette Adler in Paris in 1938, traveled to her hiding place with a man she hardly knew. Her parents had been born in Poland, and in October 1942, when it became clear that foreign-born Jews living in France ran the risk of deportation, her father found work in the French countryside as a lumberjack. Since his job was considered to be in the interest of the German economy, he was given a certificate protecting him and his family, who remained in Paris, from deportation. When the plight of the Jews in Paris worsened, and the certificate was no longer a guarantee of safety, Rosette's father decided that he must take steps to protect his daughter. He turned to a farmer who lived in the countryside near the lumber camp, and asked him to hide his little girl. The farmer talked it over with his wife, who agreed: they already had three daughters, and they'd just have one more. Rosette recalls some of her feelings:

I remember that I was told I was going to this place, and I was going to see my father, and I was going to take a train, and I was going with our neighbor. His name was Jean Raffa, and he had become friends with my father. He was a Christian. My mother could not take me, because they were afraid that she would be taken off the train because, at this time, she was wearing the Jewish star, the yellow star. So I remember going on the train with him, and I remember eating hard-boiled eggs and bread and butter. I remember being told that I was not to say that he was a friend or a neighbor. I remember being told to say that he was my father. This was very difficult for me, because I was about three and a half.

I knew only that I was going to see my father. I don't think I really realized that this is where I was going to spend a few years.

Rosette, along with Jack Goldstein and Benno Horowitz, was to become one of the hidden children.

Rosette Alder's father (on the right wearing a sleeveless shirt) in the lumber camp.

I was born in Germany, and my holocaust started in 1938. One morning, very early, a knock came on the door. Two men appeared, and told us to gather a few belongings and to come with them. We didn't have much time, about ten minutes. Instead of going to school, I was taken to prison. The men were separated from the women and children, and this was my first traumatic separation from my father. Once that prison door closed on us, it was horrible. The next morning, we were marched to a train, and, once off the train, we were marched for miles to the Polish border. The Polish government did not expect us. The German government was sending thousands of people to Poland, people of Polish origin. We were walking for miles, with soldiers pointing their guns at us. People were starting to throw away their belongings. Children got lost, one man was walking in his pajamas—he wasn't given enough time to get dressed. It was cold; he seemed to have lost his mind. Two soldiers were waiting at the border. And all we could find was one barn for a few hundred people, probably too many, filled with hay and people shouting, Don't smoke or we'll all go up in fire. A woman gave birth to twins. It was so scary. I asked my mother, Why? What is happening? And she tried to toughen me up and said, This is life. And I said to myself, This is life? How come? And I never asked that question again. I was not quite ten years old at that time. . . .

—Edith Knoll

PART TWO

IN HIDING

THREE

The choice of a hiding place was dictated by where they lived; whom they knew; their families' contacts with the non-Jewish, anti-Nazi world; and their ability to pay, if payment was required. It was, most often, a matter of chance.

A large number of children were given asylum in convents, orphanages, and boarding schools. Though some of the people associated with these institutions asked for money to cover the cost of keeping a child, most required no payment at all. They offered these children a relatively safe haven. As part of a group of predominantly Christian children, the Jewish children could more easily become invisible and were less likely to be discovered by the police, who, tipped by informers, paid occasional visits to these institutions.

Though the experiences of the Jewish children in these Christian institutions varied considerably from child to child, the basic conditions of their time in hiding were similar. They all lived in fear of discovery. They all had to be careful not to speak of their past lives and their families. They had to renounce their religious beliefs and, at least temporarily, practice another faith. And they were subject to the strict rules and regulations of an institution. They were provided with sanctuary, yet, in most cases, they were not accepted as members of the community in which they were forced to live. They were always aware of being outsiders.

Nonetheless, they were given shelter; they had beds in which to sleep; and they had food, no matter how meager at times. Most important, they were usually treated with kindness and compassion.

Edith Knoll, who now lives in Great Neck, New York, remains deeply grateful to those whose courage saved her life. Born in Germany of Polish parents, her early years were similar to those of most foreign-born German Jews. First, her family was deported and returned to Poland. Then, they were allowed to return to Germany for a few days, from which, with the help of the underground, they were smuggled to Belgium, where they hoped to live in safety. With the conquest of Belgium, however, their lives were again endangered. It was the beginning of a heartbreaking period, during which the family tried to find a new home—in Antwerp or in Brussels—and during which Edith's father was taken to prison and then sent to Auschwitz where, she later learned, he died.

Alone and desperate, Edith and her mother

Edith Knoll shortly before she was deported to Poland in 1938.

found that a doctor who had been treating Edith's mother for a skin disease was willing to help them. He first offered to take Edith into his own home, where she could become part of his family, but the young girl's mother refused to be separated from her daughter. His next suggestion—that both be placed as patients in the clinic, run by nuns, where he worked—was eagerly accepted. Unfortunately, they were only able to stay there for a few weeks. German patients, too, came to the clinic, and, fearing that they might become suspicious, the mother superior arranged for Edith and her mother to be moved to a convent outside of Brussels. Edith remembers the trip and their reception at the convent vividly:

At 5:00 in the morning, a trip to the convent. I was so scared. We were so scared. Because they could have found us. I was afraid when I heard a footstep. I was afraid of people looking at me, wondering if perhaps the next person will denounce me and that will be the end. We made it to the convent by tram and it took, not that long, but when I remembered it later, I thought it had taken hours. When we got to the convent and we were ushered into Mother Superior's office, she put her arms around us and we felt safe for a little while. She was an incredible woman. She was hiding, at the end of the war, ten Jewish adults, twenty-eight Jewish children, British parachutists, weapons, resistance fighters. She was one of the latter herself and she was decorated after the war. She kept us for almost two years.

Though constantly afraid of being caught by the Gestapo and deported, Edith's experience was less painful than it might have been because of the presence of her mother and the sympathetic treatment she received from the mother superior and the other nuns:

She was running a boarding school and we did get an education, one, more or less, that would prepare us for the future. At the age of fourteen I was concerned with how I would make a living and support my mother, and I was still hoping that somehow my father had survived and would come back—but I didn't know in what condition, and I would have to take care of him. This is at the age of fourteen, and I would spend sleepless nights. But she [the mother superior] did a very good job; she taught us practical things, aside from poetry and music, literature and history. She also gave us skills like shorthand, and I spoke several languages by the time I was twelve. I had to deal with six languages and I took shorthand in four languages; I knew how to type; I was taught bookkeeping and anything to run an office. . . .

One day, however, the Germans came to the convent, and Edith's stay there came to an end:

They were looking for British parachutists. A glove was found in one of the fields. And we were taken out of the building—I always thought it was so big, but when I went back there I realized that it wasn't. We were taken into the field and all day long we hid behind bushes, and when the Germans left, we were told to come back—the nuns were looking for us. At 5:00 in the morning, after putting a few things together by candlelight, we had to disappear. Many children were taken to orphanages—they didn't know where their parents were. And I went back with my mother to the convent clinic, where we had first been hidden, and when I rang the doorbell,

Mother Superior said, "I couldn't turn out a dog. So how could I turn you away?" She put us inside the convent—nobody ever put a foot in her place, and nobody knew about us except for three nuns. We had a staircase leading to a kitchen, and one priest would come a few times a week to tell us how the invasion went, to give us hope that the liberation was very near. And so we stayed behind these doors, in great fear.

Gisele Warshawsky who, with her mother, brother, and sister, had returned to Brussels after failing to reach England in 1940, did not become a hidden child until 1942, about the same time Edith Knoll had. By then, both her brother and sister had been deported and, she later learned, had lost their lives in the concentration camp at Auschwitz. It was after the deportation of her older son and daughter that Gisele's mother was persuaded that the time for hiding had come. Gisele remembers when and how that decision was made:

Everybody was telling my mother, You better start hiding, you better start doing something about not keeping your child in the house. We lived in a wonderful building where the people were Belgian—they were the kindest and the most compassionate toward the Jews. And they loved my mother and my family. The man that owned the garage in the back of the house, Charles De Rudder, he came to my mother after my brother and sister were taken, and he used to warn my mother not to go into the street. But we needed food, so my mother used to send me out and I would buy five pounds of potatoes, and coal to heat the house, and whatever else I could buy—my brother had left money for us. I was a child, but somehow or other, my mother always used to say, If anything happens here in this *house, if anybody comes, you run to Mr. De Rudder and he is going to take care of you. And one day she left me with another neighbor. Her name was Madame Marie, and she watched me while my mother, I found out later, was looking to hide me, because I couldn't return to school.*

Through Mr. De Rudder, Gisele's mother met a Belgian priest who undertook to find one hiding place for Gisele and another for her mother—it was thought safest that the two be separated. Gisele's hiding place was to be in a Catholic orphanage run by nuns. The orphanage housed about ninety children, among them thirty-five Jews, who were given new names and warned not to tell anyone that they were Jews. Only the mother superior and Father Benoit, who conducted Mass, knew.

Life at this particular orphanage was far more difficult than it was at most such institutions. The nuns in charge offered neither warmth nor compassion—only shelter—to these frightened children, who lived in appalling conditions.

We didn't have food. They served us bread that was very, very bad. The nuns ate good bread, but the children didn't. We sort of had the leftovers that came from a bakery in town. In the summertime, it was so bad, you couldn't eat it. It was rancid. They served us herring with worms crawling on it; we had to remove the skin and the worms in order to eat what was on the inside.

We were all very, very thin and dirty. Once a week we got a bath. And the nuns, you know, they were staunch Catholics. They took the older girls to bathe the younger children, and I tried to get in the front of the line so I could be at least the first or second one in the bathtub, because they didn't change the bathwater. But unfortu-

nately, because I was one of the younger kids, I didn't always have a chance to be first, so I'd have to bathe in dirty water.

Only two people made life easier for the children: one was Father Benoit and one a kitchen worker. Though neither had the power to make significant changes at the orphanage, Gisele remembers them both with affection:

Father Benoit used to take some of us younger children out into the field in order to give us an outing. He was very nice. I was one of the children who was very lucky to be able to get out maybe once a month. We would go to the fields in the rain and try to get berries. We would try to get strawberries just to have something to eat. We were starved—we just didn't have any food. There was, however, a young girl—I don't remember her name—who worked in the kitchen. She cooked and helped the nuns. This young woman felt so sorry for the younger children, especially the ones that were eight, nine, or ten. Once in a while she would sneak us a sandwich. She would actually give us a slice of bread, real country bread that was baked there for the nuns, and she would slice it and put a little honey on it, and butter. She had to sneak it in to us, and we would share the slice from this big loaf between two or three little girls. And that was like manna from heaven.

Gisele had kept in touch by letter with Mr. De Rudder. He had assured her that her mother was safely hidden, but she was unable to let him know of conditions at the orphanage because the mail was censored by the nuns. In the summer of 1943, however, one of the older girls managed to sneak a letter to the woman who had brought them to the orphanage. Soon this woman arrived and verified the children's complaints, assuring them that she would make arrangements to have them moved. She kept her promise: all thirty-five girls were placed elsewhere. Gisele was among twenty girls sent to a boarding school in the village of Sugny, near the Belgian border with Luxembourg, which housed about sixty children. She remained there for a year and a half. Life there contrasted sharply with that at the orphanage:

Gisele (first row, second from the left), in Sugny.

Our group arrived at a girls' boarding school called L'Institut de la Reine Elizabeth. The school had been closed several years before, at the beginning of the war. The main house was occupied by a group of nuns—several had taught at the Institut—whose services were no longer used. They were middle-aged ladies, extremely kindhearted and gentle. They were the volunteers; by doing the cooking for the children they did charitable work and performed their Christian duty to mankind. They performed many other works, such as tending the vegetable gardens which fed the school. There was even a chicken farm, which they tended, and several pigs and cows. The school was pretty self-sufficient due to these hard-working women—a different breed from the ones we had known at the orphanage.

We had to be fed, bathed, deloused, and issued new clothing. Everything brought from home by now had become outgrown. If not outgrown, clothing had been lost or given to others at the orphanage. For the first time in one and one-half years, we began to eat good healthy food (eggs, milk, meat, vegetables, etc.) and to fill our stomachs, no longer going hungry. Many of us, including me, could not tolerate the richness of good food, and we developed sores on our bodies. The good doctor who ran the school prescribed bathing every day and scrubbings with sulphur soap. How well I still remember these scrubbings I had to endure until all boils healed! We received the greatest care and kindness from these wonderful people. I will never forget that time of my life, and how happy we were at the Institut.

Gisele took comfort in the Catholic religion, and it served as an antidote to her loneliness and feelings of isolation. Through the religion and its rituals, she felt part of a group:

We still attended Mass on Sundays, but not twice a day. We also had Protestant girls in our midst who never even had to attend Mass. The Jewish girls continued to go, as we felt protected by the Catholic religion. I felt ashamed of being Jewish, and hardly mentioned it or thought myself as other than Christian. I continued to wear the medals issued to me at the orphanage even after I was reunited with my mother. They had kept me safe, and besides, they had been blessed by the pope, I had been told.

At one point, the girls began attending classes taught by two of the sisters, but because few books were available, these classes were soon discontinued. To fill their time, they made beds, peeled potatoes, and helped care for the smaller girls. For entertainment, they put on plays, made their own costumes, and had parties on holidays. The mail was not censored, and Gisele remained in touch with Mr. De Rudder, who kept assuring her that her mother was well. Gisele felt safe, sheltered from the threat of the Nazis by caring and compassionate Christians.

In some ways, Frank Siegel's experience paralleled that of Gisele Warshawsky. After his family's failed attempt to reach England, they, too, were forced to resign themselves to living in Belgium under the oppressive restrictions of the Nazis. And later he, too, was able to move from a difficult existence at one orphanage to a far more comfortable one at a country home.

Frank Siegel with his parents in Brussels in 1941.

The time to go into hiding came in 1942, as it did for Gisele, when Frank's mother was taken to a hospital and his father, unable to care for him, sent him to live temporarily in the home of a widow who gave shelter to orphaned children. It was the last Frank saw of his mother, who was seized from her hospital room by the Gestapo and taken to Auschwitz, where she was gassed.

Before long, Frank's father realized it was necessary to find a more permanent place in which to hide his son, and he contacted a religious organization run by priests who placed children in orphanages in order to protect them. Through this organization it was arranged to have the ten-year-old boy sent to a Catholic orphanage at Namur, not far from Brussels.

Frank hated his stay at the orphanage, and despised the regimentation there. Living in a huge dormitory with the rest of the children, about ten percent of whom were Jewish and the rest orphans of the war, he had recurrent nightmares and began to wet the bed. His memories of life there are bitter:

I was always hungry, always hungry. I mean, we ate just barely enough to live. We wanted white bread, not the grain bread they gave us. We wanted chocolate too. I had forgotten what the taste of chocolate was. I even forgot what citrus fruits were like, or bananas. I didn't know what they were when the war ended and I started eating those things again. We ate basically breads, heavy soups, a little bit of meat, a lot of rutabagas. My God, did we eat rutabagas! Beets.

There came a time where we didn't wear shoes anymore. We wore wooden clogs. They seem so cute, but believe me, wearing them is a pain, because they're not tight. They bounce back and forth when you walk.

We had lay teachers in the orphanage, not nuns. They just did the administration, the discipline and things like that. They used to kick us out in the middle of the winter with shorts, and we had to play outside. I remember those winters. The winter of '43, my God, it was murder because we had no coal. There was no coal, no nothing. During that time, I got these blotches. There were scars all over my legs. That was malnutrition.

As was the case with Gisele and many of these children, Frank found comfort in one aspect of his life there. The practice of Catholicism gave him a sense of belonging.

My gosh, I didn't know what a Catholic was. I started going to Mass every day. I didn't know. I had seen these huge churches, but you don't analyze things when you are a little boy. I remember being on my knees, and the guy next to me says, "You see over there, there's this box where they put the chalice, you know," and he says, "Christ is in there." And I couldn't figure out how they got a whole body in this little box. I was a good student. I was No. 1 in catechism. They asked me if the pope was infallible. I said, Of course he isn't infallible! I wrote a long essay, justifying my position. Of course, I flunked that one. Little by little, I began to understand the Catholic religion, and actually wanted to be converted. After all, it looked pretty good.

A priest would sometimes take Frank to Brussels to visit his father for two or three days. During these visits, he spoke of his life at the orphanage, and in late 1943, his father arranged to have him moved to a home in the town of Ciney, south of Brussels.

Life at this second hiding place was far better than that at the orphanage. At first the boys, almost all of them Jewish, lived in fear of raids by German patrols that were searching for members of the Belgian underground. Later, as the war approached their area, they were frightened by the prospect of air raids. Nonetheless, conditions were relatively good. The home, set on a few acres in a beautiful part of the country, had once been the private residence of a wealthy Belgian. Today, Frank remembers it as a kind of summer camp. There was one director in charge, and a number of young women—nineteen, twenty, or twenty-one years old— who acted as monitors. Because the home was in the midst of farm country, meals, served to the boys at elongated tables, were abundant. Though they had no pillows, sleeping conditions were good. It was, he remembers, "good country living," although, without a mother and father, it was not home.

In the spring of 1942, the parents of Rachelle Goldstein also decided it was time to send their children into hiding. The increased pace of the deportations of Jews from Belgium to concentration camps made them fear for Rachelle and her brother. Arrangements were made to have them taken to an orphanage on the outskirts of Brussels; it was a Protestant orphanage, rare in Belgium, a Catholic country. Not yet three years old at the time, Rachelle remembers sleeping in an attic and she remembers the food— "basically a liquid broth, a yellow liquid, with one solitary little carrot swimming in there." But she was not unhappy there. She didn't feel abandoned or alone: her older brother, who acted as her protector, was there, as were two of her cousins. The abnormal seemed normal to her. All the other children there were also without parents, so there was no reason for her to believe that life should be otherwise. She felt alone, however, on her third birthday, when she was sick:

I had something, I don't know what, mumps or whatever. My aunt came to visit her own children, and she brought chocolate pudding from my mother, and that was an enormous treat. I remember that. I was in isolation at the time—they put me in a separate room because I was sick—so I didn't even see my aunt. Someone just came in and handed me the chocolate pudding, and said, This is from your mother. And I remember sitting there, eating my chocolate pudding with tears running down my face.

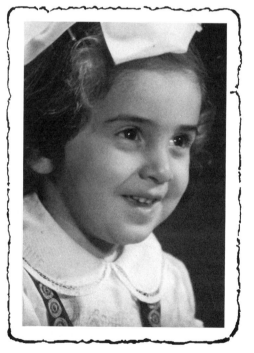

Rachelle Silberman Goldstein, age 2½, just before she was sent to a Protestant orphanage.

Rachelle's stay at the orphanage came to an abrupt end. One of the girls who lived there ran away and threatened to denounce all the Jewish girls if anyone tried to catch her and bring her back to the orphanage. All the Jewish children were sent home at once. Home, however, was no longer a safe place to be, and Rachelle remained there only until arrangements could be made to send her to another hiding place. This time, her mother contacted Père Bruno, the courageous monk who had helped Jack Goldstein. With his assistance, Rachelle was sent to a Franciscan convent—which also ran a nursery school—near Bruges, in northern Belgium. For the first time, she was on her own, separated from her brother and cousins, who were sent to a convent that took in older children. Rachelle spent a year and a half at the Franciscan convent. Unlike other children, she found no comfort in the new religion she was forced to practice:

We started off praying in the morning. I remember the room where we had to wash. It had a lot of little sinks, and it was very, very clinical-looking. White tile, cold water—there was no hot water. I remember dressing and then going to church. I remember not enjoying church very much. I didn't like having to sit with my knees on the kneeling stools. They were made of rush, which would dig into my knees. And I remember I would complain because we had bare knees, and then I'd get yelled at. I got a good indoctrination. They used to say that Jesus died on the cross because of your sins, and here you are complaining because of this. The thing that got to me was that was the first time I heard the word sin. *That was the main feature of the speech of the day. The word* sin *appeared in every other sentence, and I didn't know what* sin *meant. I remember ask-*

ing, What's a sin? So everything seemed to be a sin as I remember. I didn't know what they were talking about. . . .

After church, they would take us down into the garden and there was a path with crosses—there's a name for that, the stations of the cross or something—and we had to go and kneel again. So from kneeling in church to kneeling out there, summer or winter, it made no difference, and in the cold with bare knees. And, of course, in the garden they had little pebbles and stuff for you to kneel on. I just remember it being unpleasant.

All hidden children eagerly awaited the end of the war, though some, like Rachelle, were too young to understand exactly what that would mean:

People would always be talking to me about "before the war." The phrase before the war *was constant. Everybody always said it, and I remember going to people saying, What is it? What was it like before the war? And people would go into it. Their eyes would suddenly light up, and they would say, Oh, before the war, it was paradise. And I would say, What do you mean, what was it? They would say, Oh, we had . . . And then they would go into rhapsodies of all the things they had. I didn't know what they were talking about. I had absolutely no idea of what they were talking about. They would talk about after the war, and say, We will have all these things again. I couldn't wait to live through whatever it was we were going through and have all the things these people were talking about. I just didn't know what they were.*

During the year and a half she lived there, Rachelle never left the convent. Like the other hidden children who took refuge in institutions, she missed the warmth and affection of normal relationships more than she missed a comfortable bed or a good, satisfying meal.

I hadn't seen normal people. People to me came as priests, nuns, or lay women. I wasn't quite sure about adults and families—a lot of things didn't make sense to me. I didn't understand relationships, although I had a very, very vivid memory of my mother. I remembered that my mother had held me, and this is what kept me going. I used to dream about being held by my mother again. They had basically stripped me of all my clothes when I got there, and I had a little smock that all the kids wore. The only thing that I kept of my own was a little blue coat, and my blue coat became a security blanket. I would call it my friend, mon ami. This was the only thing I had of my own, this and my shoes, which I wore for one and a half years.

I couldn't visualize my parents anymore. I tried to picture them and I couldn't. All I could remember was the feel of them, the touch. This was an institution where people didn't touch the kids. We weren't physically abused, but there was a certain amount of mental abuse—but they didn't know any better, I guess. They were basically ignorant, the lay women who took care of us. The nuns were very distant; they were busy in prayers all day. They had very little to do with us. I remember once I was actually smacked because I was walking and my shoelace had opened up, and a nun bent down to tie my shoelace. The woman who took care of us there got highly incensed by this,

Rachelle at a Franciscan convent near Bruges in 1944.

that a nun had bent down to tie my shoelaces, so she gave me a few good smacks. I mean, it was an institution. It did bother me that some of the kids went home. The other thing that they did which really, really bothered me, which makes me angry to this day, was at night. They wanted us to go to sleep quietly and not talk to each other, etc., so they would have this little masquerade every night. They would knock loudly on the dormitory door to warn us that they were coming in.

Hidden children also worried that their families might not survive the war. They feared, too, that those parents who had survived might never find their children. Since many children had been put into the care of strangers, children worried that parents might have no idea of their whereabouts. Rachelle shared this anxiety:

I was absolutely devastated over this. I kept on saying, They'll never find me. How will they find me? And they [the priests and nuns] kept on assuring me, They'll come after the war, they'll find you. And I kept saying, They can't! How will they find me? They didn't bring me here. How do they know where I am? And they would assure me that they'll find you, they'll find you. I remember worrying about it all the time at night. How would they find me? Also, I knew they were in a place called Brussels. And when there were bombings, there would be so many planes that everything shook when they went over us. All the windows were always taped to prevent them from shaking, so they would not shatter when there was a bombing. People would say, Don't worry, they are going to bomb Brussels, they are not coming here. And then I would really worry. That really disturbed me.

Jack Goldstein, who also found sanctuary in a Belgian convent shared many of Rachelle's feelings. Each morning he was required to join the other boys, some of whom were merely boarded there by their parents, in church. Though he spent the day there studying Christianity, he never forgot that he was a Jew. When he prayed silently, he recited the Hebrew prayer he had learned by heart. The nine-year-old boy never blamed God for his situation; he just prayed to him for the salvation of his parents.

Basically, what I prayed for is that my parents would survive. That was my big worry. I mean, here we were. I didn't know where they were, what was going on. Of course we had the love for them and to lose them— And what would happen to us? We were nine years old and having to be raised as Christians. Would we just stay in this convent? The future didn't seem really bright.

There wasn't much food at the convent, and at most meals the children ate hot cereal and, perhaps, a piece of bread. But what Jack missed most, in spite of the care and compassion of the priests who sheltered him, was his parents:

Sunday was tough, because a lot of the children were visited by their parents. I was very envious of the other children. It really hurt, it was really painful to see whatever they brought them. In Belgium everything was rationed, but their parents brought them some food, some books, and I was envious. The big thing on Sunday, for us who weren't able to see our parents, was they'd give us sardines, which I thought was the biggest treat ever. They'd give you some bread, and you could dip the bread in the oil, and it was a very, very big treat to have these sardines on Sundays.

Klemak Nowicki, another of the children who took refuge in a convent, shares Jack's gratitude for his rescuers. Today a psychologist in New York City, Klemak was born in 1937 in Stanislawow, Poland, on the eastern border between Poland and Russia. Together with his parents and his grandparents, the young boy lived in a ghetto until, armed with forged baptismal papers his father obtained for them, he, his mother, and his grandmother managed to escape the roundup of Jews that inevitably led to death. Both his father and grandfather, who had stayed behind, had, he learned later, died in a concentration camp.

During the months that followed, the three fugitives went from home to home, seeking a safe refuge. In the course of their moves, the boy's grandmother was betrayed by a neighbor, captured, and killed by the Gestapo. Finally, desperate, Klemak's mother decided it was time to send her son away to a hiding place. Separately, they would have a better chance of avoiding recognition and capture. She turned for help to a bishop of a Catholic church. Klemak remembers:

We ran out in darkness, and went to this church that my mother heard about. She had heard about this bishop who apparently was friendly to the Jews. She placed herself at his mercy. She was at the end of her rope—exhausted. She told him exactly who she was. She figured it was a last-chance effort. She couldn't run anymore. So she confessed to him, and told him exactly who she was, and who I was, and so on. And he in fact did hide Jews. There were a couple of hundred Jews hiding in the basement of his church, which was extraordinarily brave of him, because he could have been killed for doing this. Now that's not common. It's a rarity. But there were a *lot of righteous Christians. The bishop was that kind of person. He said he realized that my mother's survival was contingent upon not being with me. I was a dead giveaway. He suggested a convent outside of Warsaw.*

Klemak's mother accompanied her son on the train ride to the convent. Their reception there was a warm one:

There was a young nun who was extremely kind and showed my mother around the place, and asked her if it was okay, was it good enough. She knew we were Jewish. A retired bishop was living there, and he, too, knew I was a Jew. The people in the convent knew I was a Jew. She asked my mother if she thought this was good enough for me. My mother began to cry, because it was beautiful. It was clean. It was safe. Mother was grateful just for a safe place, much less a clean one. They had, I think, mostly boys. There were thirty kids in the convent, only three Jews. The rest were orphans or Christian kids who were placed there by their parents for safety's sake until the war ended. There weren't bunks, there were big halls full of beds.

Klemak remained in the convent for almost three years. During the first year, his mother visited him every Sunday. Most of the time, she would bring him food, usually a hard-boiled egg and an apple, even though food was increasingly scarce as the war progressed. While he remembers little of his daily life at the convent, he remembers going to confession and saying the blessing at mealtimes: "I assimilated very quickly to being a Catholic, not because they forced me, but because it was part of a general plan for me to hide."

FOUR

The Jewish children who were able to remain in convents, orphanages, and boarding schools were, in many ways, among the most fortunate. They were guaranteed some kind of food and shelter and had access, when needed, to medical care. Even if most of them considered themselves outsiders, they were a part of a group of other children—they had companionship and the possibility of making friends. Furthermore, though they were removed from their familiar surroundings, they were shielded from the outside world and from some of the deprivations and dangers that most civilians experienced during the war.

No statistics are available concerning the number of Jewish children who found sanctuary in institutions compared with those who were hidden elsewhere. Yet it is reasonable to assume that the majority of the children who were forced to become invisible were hidden in private homes.

A small number managed to hide with their families in temporary homes of their own, generally in remote, isolated areas where the chances of discovery were small. Benno Horowitz, today a dentist in Washington, D.C., was among these. Together with his mother, his younger brother, and his father, who had been arrested by the police but had managed to escape, he found safety in a wooden chalet in the French Alps. The family was able to remain there until the liberation of France.

Benno at the farm in 1943.

Throughout this period, they were forced to hide their identities. Their neighbors and the farmer who arranged for them to stay at the chalet never suspected that they were Jewish. The Horowitzes said that Benno's German-born mother, who spoke French with a German accent (as do many French citizens of Alsace) was an Alsatian who feared being taken by the Germans and made a German citizen. They also said that she was a widow, and that the man she lived with was not her husband and the father of the two boys, but was instead her Romanian boyfriend who had to be hidden because of his illegal status in the country.

Benno and his brother worked in the fields, and they felt reasonably secure at first, when the Italian army, allies of the Germans, occupied the region. The Italians paid little attention to them. But when the Germans took over, they lived in fear of a raid, as the Germans relentlessly searched for hidden Jews or for any young men who could be sent to Germany to work in the factories. Benno, an adolescent, was able to sleep soundly only during snowstorms, when the chalet was impossible to reach, for the Germans would certainly have taken him away if they had discovered him.

The family took one precaution—they asked the farmer to build a hiding place within the chalet where they might be safe if the Germans came. Benno remembers it:

We had him build a double wall that we could all slip inside if we had to. You couldn't see it, it had a hidden door with the same wood. However, that wood was fresh—it hadn't been weathered and tanned from the sun—and it was my job to stain it to make the color match. I finally ended up buying tea on the black market—it was hard to find because it was imported, but we found some. And I could stain the wood to match the rest, with tea of a certain strength. One day we used the hiding place—not I nor my brother nor my mother, but my father. We were constantly on the lookout, and that day we saw Germans coming toward us on a little path at the bottom of the hill. They were coming toward our chalet, so he slipped behind the double wall. He was trembling, he was petrified with fear. After he slipped in, we could not see him anymore. He locked himself in—he wouldn't even let us boys in, he was so afraid to open the door. But, as it happens, the Germans had come to get butter and eggs at the farm; they hadn't come for us. They stood at the back door, and they didn't come into the house.

The chalet in which Benno and his family lived.

In spite of the danger of discovery, Benno and his brother were lucky: they stayed together in their own home. Far more Jewish children were forced to hide in the homes of Christian families. Risking their own lives, most of these families welcomed the children into their homes, provided them with new identities, and protected them until the war came to an end. Other families, the minority, took in these young children only in order to earn some money. They preferred girls to boys, as boys, because of circumcision, were easily recognizable as Jews. And, not acting for humanitarian reasons, they treated these children well only as long as they were paid. If the parents of the children were no longer able to pay—and it was not unusual for them to run out of money—the initial kindness and generosity of the hosts turned to anger and resentment. They no longer wanted to keep the children, but they were afraid to turn them out, fearing that the authorities might then learn that they had sheltered the enemy and punish them accordingly. Some of these families resigned themselves to the presence of these unwelcome guests, while others became abusive.

Each hidden child has a different story to tell. Some were treated well, and some were not; some of the hidden children managed to remain with the same family, while others were forced by circumstances to move from family to family, from home to home.

Rosette Goldstein, today the food service manager at a Long Island, New York, bank, was among the former, spending her years in hiding at the farm where she had been taken by a neighbor. She remembers her arrival there, near the camp in the French countryside where her father worked as a lumberjack:

All of a sudden I found myself on this farm with these people. My father came that night, because he was allowed to come in the evening. He had a bicycle, and he used to bicycle over. He was there that first night, so I felt pretty safe. The next thing I knew, well, they used to keep cider bottles on the table, because that's the way the French farmers were—they would be thirsty and they would drink cider. So this little girl was thirsty, and they thought nothing of it. I drank quite a bit, and I can remember being very happy and dancing all over the place that night. I don't remember being put to sleep or anything, but the next morning, everybody was gone. Our neighbor had gone back to Paris, and my father had gone to work. And here I was with strangers, people I really didn't know. There were three daughters in the family. The youngest was fourteen years old, and I slept with her in one bed.

Rosette's father came to visit her every night, and she remembers running down a long driveway to meet him as soon as she heard the sound of his whistle. It was far more difficult for her mother to come to see her, and when she finally did, it was a dramatic visit:

She somehow got to the farm and came to see us. My father stayed at the farm that night. The next morning, instead of going back to the camp, he went straight to the forest to work. And all of a sudden there were these men at the farm, with rifles. I don't think they were dressed as soldiers. They came in, and they asked where my father was. Evidently, they had all this information. They saw my mother and me, and they said my father had deserted, because by that time this company was working for the German interest. . . . They were in the farmhouse; I can still see it. They said to my mother that if my father wasn't back within one hour, they would take my mother and me. Mr. Martin, the farmer, took his bicycle and went to the woods where my father was working, and told him. He immediately went back to the camp.

Rosette's mother returned to Paris at once. The young girl never saw her father again, and learned later that he had been sent to Drancy, near Paris, and from there to Auschwitz and on to a labor camp, where he died.

Made to feel, as much as possible, a part of the Martin family, she was nonetheless alone:

I can't say that I suffered, but I remember feeling very lonely. I had no friends. I didn't go to school. I was little. As I said, they were

Rosette (on the right) with Mrs. Martin and her youngest daughter.

good to me, but . . . For instance, the youngest girl, who was fourteen years old, was very jealous, and I remember one night being in bed, and she was angry with me—probably I must have done something and maybe she got blamed for it, I don't know. And she said to me, You're a dirty little Jew. I was too young to understand exactly what that meant. I knew I was different, but I didn't know how. I was going to church every Sunday with them, but they wouldn't let me go to catechism. I was not allowed to go, but I went to church. And I wanted to go. I was, you know, a little girl. So I remember that when she said that to me in bed, I said, You are a dirty Jew.

But other than that, I can't remember them ever being nasty to me. They were very, very good to me. . . . But I can remember being very fright-

ened and lonely, oh God, very lonely. Very lonely. I mean, I called them Mr. and Mrs. Martin. And the girls, the older ones who were working in the fields, they were busy making cheese and milking cows and all that—they had no time for me. The younger one used to have to watch the cows, and I would go with her. We would be gone the whole day, sitting in the field with cows, just the two of us, no toys.

They used to dry pumpkin seeds. There were chicken coops, low chicken coops. And on top of the chicken coops, they used to dry these pumpkin seeds. This is what I played with; these were my toys. The other thing that was very interesting to do was to go to the fields when the planes used to drop propaganda papers. I would go with a little basket and pick up these papers, because we had no paper, no toilet paper, and this is what it was used for.

There was always enough fresh food to eat, and there were the pleasures of living in a small community.

We always had food because it was a farm. There were chickens. We made our own butter. We made our own soap. I could even tell you how to make soap. We used to go and pick fruit. They used to grow wheat. All the neighbors would come when we would kill a hog to put away for the winter, you know, the whole neighborhood would come, and it would be very festive, because all of this meat had to be cured and prepared. And so we would all get together. We did the same thing when we would get the grapes to make wine. There were a lot of people together, and everybody did it, and everybody did it at different farms. Everybody helped each other.

Alice Sondike, born Alicja Melcer in Warsaw in October 1939, one month after the Germans had marched into Poland, spent her time in three different homes during the Holocaust. Today she lives in East Norwich, New York. At the time of her birth, there were four hundred thousand Jews in Warsaw (approximately one-third of the city's population), 250,000 of whom lived in a predominantly Jewish section. On October 3, 1940, the German governor of Warsaw announced that all Jews living outside of that section would have to move there at once, bringing with them only as many personal belongings as they could carry. Warsaw was to be divided into three districts—German, Polish, and Jewish. In Poland, Jews were never called Polish or Polish Jews—they were thought of simply as Jews. These Jews would be crowded into an area that measured less than 2.5 percent of the area of the total city. On November 15, the Warsaw ghetto, in which the Jews were forcibly assembled, was officially declared to be in existence.

While the Melcers were living in the ghetto, Alice's mother made contact with a young Jewish friend who passed as a Christian and lived outside the ghetto, working to help the Jews. Together they spoke of sending Alice to live, disguised as a Christian, with a Polish family. It was not an easy decision for her parents to make:

Alicja Melcer (Alice Sondike) and her mother.

They thought about it very long and hard, and it was a lot to decide at this point because they didn't know what to do. Unlike others, they knew what was going to happen. They knew there was going to be more and worse. My grandparents had already been taken. My aunt had been taken with

one of the children. So they decided that they would send me away.
A family was found, a Christian family who were Communists and
who said they would take me. And one day, my mother's friend came
into the ghetto, and walked out with me. My first memories are of
living with this Christian family. I was with other families subse-
quently, but my first memories are there.

The people who first sheltered Alice were good people, among
the "righteous Gentiles." The young girl suffered the inevitable
effects of the war, but no more so than did her rescuers. They
were as good to her as they were to their own five-year-old son,
who knew that Alice was a Jew but never revealed her true identity to the neighbors. These latter believed that the little girl's father was a soldier in the Polish army and that her mother was
dead. After the war, many years later, Alice learned that the same
family that had sheltered her had been hiding another Jewish
family in their basement at the same time, and that they had
even offered to hide Alice's mother. Alice's mother rejected this
offer "because she felt she would jeopardize my state by being
there, since if they got angry with me for any reason, they would
think twice about sending a child out alone, but if the child's
mother was also there, they would send both of us out."

Unfortunately, Alice's stay with this family came to an end after
little more than a year. The neighbors began to have their doubts
about her story, and it was decided that she should be moved to
the country, to the home of relatives of her first hosts. The stay
with this second family was a short one. For reasons that were
never explained to her, Alice was soon sent to live with a German
couple. They also lived in the country, and they agreed to take her

in because, childless, they wanted a child of their own. The second couple with whom Alice had stayed knew that she was Jewish, as had the previous family. However, the Germans, with whom she remained until the end of the war, never suspected that they were sheltering a Jew.

For the first time, Alice was without companions and without the warmth and affection she had come to feel were normal.

The two of them worked all day. I was basically locked in the house while they were gone. I guess I must have been about four years old. I took whatever there was to eat. I took a nap at the same time every day. I played alone in the house for the whole time I was there. There were children outside, because I remember looking through the window, and you know, to this day, I still have that habit. I stand by a window and I look. But there were children outside who I would wave to and who would wave to me. I don't know what they thought. But no one ever came to the house. They probably thought I was sick, that I wasn't allowed to come out.

Alice remembers the couple who took her in with bitterness.

They were not good people. They were abusive people. He was, you know, I wouldn't call it a spanker. I would call it more a hitter. She was a typical German housewife who just didn't have any say in the matter. I think basically she was a kind, decent person, but she didn't have any feelings about standing up for your child. And this would have been my lot in life. I could have been with them for the rest of my life. They had been promised that if my parents didn't come back, if my father didn't come back . . . At that time, there was no question that my mother was dead. But if my father didn't come back, they could adopt me. And this is what they were waiting for— the end of the war when all the soldiers would come back.

Rosette Goldstein was able to remain in one home during her years in hiding, while Alice Sondike found three places of asylum. The experiences of Stefanie Seltzer, who today lives in a Main Line community outside of Philadelphia, were typical of those of very many hidden children. She spent the war going from one hiding place to another, moving at least seven times during those dangerous years.

Stefanie, born in Lodz, Poland, in 1938, was raised in the ghetto of the town of Radomsko. She was an only child. Her parents, foreseeing the danger that would face all the Jews of Poland, felt it would be difficult enough to hide one child—that it would be unfair to bring more children into the world.

Stefanie spent the entire war in Poland. At first, her mother arranged to have her smuggled out of the ghetto and taken to the country by Wanda, a prostitute, whose mother and son lived in a small village in the countryside. Given a new name, she pretended to be Wanda's illegitimate child who had been raised elsewhere. She was unable to remain there for long, however. When it seemed likely that the truth might be discovered, the four-year-old girl was taken back to Warsaw. Her mother had been in a coma for two weeks following severe hemorrhaging from a bleeding ulcer and was so weakened and disfigured by her illness that Stefanie was unable at first to recognize her.

Mother and daughter sought refuge together in the home of the non-Jewish wife of a relative; Stephanie doesn't know just what the relationship was. The woman sympathized with their plight:

We went there to find someone to feed us; my mother again was not well. She gave my mother her own bed, and shared food with us. This woman's husband worked for the underground army in London. He was a scientist. And her daughter, who was eighteen, worked for the Polish underground. We stayed there for a while and she was very, very good to us. Eventually she gave us a room in the basement, and my mother had to lie flat on her back, because they felt that if she moved too much or got up she would start the hemorrhaging again.

During her stay there, Stefanie had to assume many of the responsibilities of an adult.

I became sort of the breadwinner for a while. There was a man who lived on a very wide street, and there was a strip of plantings and flowers separating the two sides of the street. During the war, this man, who was very enterprising, had taken these gardens, dug them up and planted vegetables. I worked for him, weeding. As a child you can do that, you are closer to the ground. During that time, I earned some potatoes. I would work all day and he would give me potatoes and carrots, sometimes cucumbers. I remember my mother didn't trust me to peel the potatoes. For some reason, she didn't peel them. I remember that I would cook them on this little burner and then, when they were cooked, I would bring them over to my mother, and she would get the skins off. We lived on that. Occasionally he would give me some milk. But this woman was very good to us.

Unfortunately, for reasons she never knew, Stefanie and her mother soon had to leave. She has memories of some of the hiding places that followed. She vividly remembers one house, across the street from the Warsaw ghetto, where she was hidden by a woman she called Aunt Lucia. Her mother had found a job as a housemaid and was able to pay the small rent that Lucia asked. During her time there, Stefanie could not go out into the streets alone because she lacked the identity papers that residents were required to carry. She lived on the third floor:

It was a very, very old, decrepit house with bedbugs. Every night, before we went to bed, the woman would boil water, and we would throw it on the walls, hoping to discourage some of the bedbugs, but it didn't really help. I had completely open sores everywhere. As for the apartment, you walked in and there was a bathroom, just a toilet on the right-hand side, but the plumbing wasn't working in this old house, so everything had to be carried down. There were only two rooms, and this woman sublet—she had an old, old woman who was paying her something to live with her, and this woman's niece and nephew lived with her, and her brother who worked for the Gestapo also lived there. In the first room, there was a table in the middle of the room, a dining table, and it had a very long tablecloth—in those days you had long tablecloths that went to the floor—and there was a little stool under the table. When her brother who worked for the Gestapo would come, he was, fortunately, often drunk. He would sit at the end where the table was. I would be under the table, and he would be sitting in a chair against the wall. Sometimes he would be there two or three days, and I could not come out from under the table. Even though he was drunk, he might notice me.

There was little food. Stefanie had no ration card, so, apart from the food her mother was able to steal for her from the house where she worked, the young child had to live on the limited amount that Lucia could give her from her own rations:

Our diet at that time consisted mostly of just black bread, and there was black oil, the unrefined oil. So most of my diet just consisted of that. Fortunately, at that point, I loved cod-liver oil. I absolutely loved it. So it was on my steady diet. You hear about the cafeteria diet, that children will eat what the body needs. I guess my body needed it. I was totally mad for it. I also remember I had sore throats quite a lot, and in those days they dipped this thing which looked like a large Q-Tip in iodine, and they slapped your throat with it, and it kept you more or less healthy, I guess, but I did suffer a lot of sore throats then. But I was also so malnourished, and I had all these infected bites, and I was under the table quite a bit of the time. I couldn't even go to the window, because someone might see me.

Stefanie also remembers another hiding place, in the villa of a Jewish woman married to a non-Jew. The woman, whose boyfriend was a highly placed member of the Gestapo and could warn her of any police raids, had hidden between fifteen and twenty Jews at one point or another.

While staying at the villa, Stefanie learned the advantages of being a girl:

At one point—I don't know how I got them—I did have papers, and my mother would leave me during the day to go to the hospital,

where she then worked as an operating room nurse. There was a lit-
tle boy there with his mother—he was about my age, but he had no
papers. He had black curly hair, very beautiful. The danger for boys
was even greater than for girls, because of circumcision. So this lit-
tle boy had been taught to speak as a girl. He was my age, my size,
and he wore my dresses, so that if he was seen, no one would know
he was a boy. We were in hiding then, and he certainly had no pa-
pers and he couldn't leave, but I guess he was being taught that,
just in case he ever had to come out and someone would speak to
him, he was to speak as a girl.

Most of the homes in which the hidden children were placed remained just as they had been before the war—simple residences where space, usually just an extra bed, was found for a hidden child. Because the villa in which Stefanie was hidden had been used as a hiding place for many Jews, it had been carefully prepared for its "guests." Stefanie recalls two areas in the house that were used for hiding in case of emergency:

One was in the basement. There was a toilet in the basement.
They removed the tank from the wall, and they made a hole behind
the tank that you could crawl into. An underground passage had
been dug out that led to the next house. That was in case you had
to go into hiding. That was one area.

And another hiding place was up in the top floor. There was a
small room with a bed, and behind the bed was a little cabinet. It
had two shelves, and there were bottles there. If you removed the
bottles and if you removed one shelf, there was a keyhole behind the
shelf. And if you opened up the back of that cabinet, you could

crawl one by one into the eaves of this villa. You know how a roof drops off? You could crawl into that space in the eaves, and there was enough space to accommodate all the people in the house.

She has not forgotten one unusual incident, when two members of the Gestapo arrived unexpectedly at the house. Their protector's boyfriend had either not known of the raid or had not had time to warn them:

As it happens, my mother was in the house that day. Even though she had papers and I had papers, she panicked and she took me, and we all went into this one crawl space in the eaves of the house. I guess there wasn't really room, and there wasn't time to get into the lower crawl space because the Gestapo were already on the bottom floor. Everybody crowded in there. It was a very, very terrible day. Soon after we had gotten into that hiding place in the eaves of the house, we could hear the boots of the Gestapo men in that little room. She had closed it up after us, but you could hear the Gestapo boots. And all the adults in the space started to laugh and speak loudly and say, We don't have to worry anymore—it's all over. Speak as loudly as you wish. Do whatever you like, it's all over, it's okay, speak loudly.

They laughed very, very loudly and shouted to each other. It was absolutely horrible. This little boy and I went from person to person, and we put our hands over their mouths and we said, Please don't make any noise. We had been taught not to make any noise. So we said, Please don't make any noise because we want to live, and if you make all of this noise, they will hear us and we won't be able to live, and we want to live. And they didn't calm down. I guess eventually they quieted down somewhat, but they had been very, very noisy. Later we heard the boots retreating again, and nobody had opened up that space. The woman later told us she saw the Gestapo out the door. There were two of them. She said that she had, of course, heard all the noise, but I guess there were two Gestapo men who just didn't want to know that there were people hidden in that house.

Some Jewish children were even less fortunate than those who found refuge in the homes of strangers. These children, for months or even years, lived in airless basements, cramped attics, or barns without light. Fran Greene and Roald Hoffmann were among these.

Fran Greene, who now lives in Jericho, New York, was born Fela Frost in Lukow, a small Polish village near Lublin. She thinks she was born in 1935, but she's not certain; no one has been able to tell her. She does, however, remember the arrival of the Germans in her village, and she knows she was a very small child then— Poland was invaded by the Nazis in September 1939:

I *don't know the exact date, but I do remember when the Germans came in. It's like a dream that I can still see right in front of my eyes. I remember seeing these humongous people on horses, and the town was burning, and things were happening. It doesn't really seem real, but yet I can see it right now, that this actually happened in that manner.*

And she remembers that when she was three or four years old, her father paid a farmer and his family to hide her:

He put me with this family that had many children. It was not a very good time for me, because I was used to being just one of two children and, you know, eating wasn't like family-style. I remember I ate nothing, and the people were very nervous about keeping me there, and they were right. When someone came to visit, they would put me on top of the oven. They used the oven for heating and cooking. It was pretty warm there, but they would hide me up there. Sometimes people stayed a long time, and it was a very terrible experience.

Before very long, her father arranged to move her to a nearby barn, where she was reunited with other members of her family:

He arranged for our whole family to be hidden underneath. A bunker was built underneath the barn, and it was covered with straw or whatever, right underneath, in the earth. They were proficient at that because the refrigeration, I think, was done that way, underneath. I can't really remember what it looked like, but there was bedding there. It was myself, my brother, my parents, and my paternal grandparents, and we stayed there some time. I don't know how long a time. My father, a young man, used to go out. One time he got caught, and he was put on

Fela Frost (Fran Greene) and her parents.

the train to Treblinka. He jumped off the train, and this young man jumped off with him, and he brought him when he came back to us. Each time he would go out, he would come back with some food and some news, I guess. I was too young to really be interested in what was happening. But still I was surrounded by my loved ones. My brother was very young, he must have just been a baby.

Fran believes that the family must have remained there for about two years, barely eking out an existence. Toward the end of the war, however, they were forced to flee:

One time when my father had come back from some place, he heard something outside. So he went outside to see what was happening, and he did not return. Then my mother decided to go see where he went, and she went out, and she didn't return. I must have been a precocious little girl. I just tore myself away from my grandparents, and I ran upstairs to see where they went. I went outside, and there was snow, and I saw them running away, and I ran after them. We ran away, and my father took us somewhere to someone, and he hid us inside some straw; they used to have these big bales for feed for the animals. It was used for different things, and we hid inside.

The three of them were unable to remain there, however. They moved to a different place—most often a barn—almost every night. Later they learned of the massacre that took place after they left the first barn.

We later found out that they burned our barn. They killed my grandparents. My grandparents were burned. My little brother was shot because he ran out. They killed the farmer. And they were Poles, Polish people. Recently I found out that they had first gone to another place, looking for Jews, just to kill Jews. When they arrived at that place, the Jews had already gone away. So the owner said, There's nobody here. But they were pushing him and hurting him, and he said, Go and visit my brother. And apparently that's how they found us, because they hadn't really known we were there.

Roald Hoffmann, who lives in Ithaca, New York, was, in 1981, awarded the Nobel Prize in chemistry. He spent fifteen months of his childhood hiding in an attic. He has few precise memories of those months; he gives voice to those memories through his moving, heartfelt poetry, much of which has been published.

Born in 1937, in Zloczow, Poland, his real name was not Hoffmann—the name given on his papers after the war—but Safran. His father was Hillel Safran and his mother, Clara May Rosen. The history of the town of his birth is complicated. Between the two world wars, Zloczow, situated in the Ukraine, was a part of Poland; and in September 1939, it was annexed by the Soviet Union. Its population of thirty thousand was then divided about equally among Ukrainians, Poles, and Jews.

The Soviet occupation ended in the summer of 1941, when Germany invaded the U.S.S.R. and shortly afterward occupied Zloczow. Everything quickly changed. The Ukrainians went on a rampage that lasted three days. In that short time, an estimated three thousand Jews were murdered, among them one of Roald's grandparents. The Jews who survived were put into a ghetto and then into nearby labor camps.

Roald's father, a civil engineer, was useful to the firm that had been hired by the Germans to reconstruct the war-damaged bridges and roads, and his life was spared initially. He continued to work and to move about freely while his wife and son lived in a labor camp. In September 1942, however, the situation again changed. The German army, which had invaded the Soviet Union, was stopped at the city then known as Stalingrad. It was a turning point in the war, and many Poles and Ukrainians realized for the first time that the Nazis were not invincible. It became clear to them that the Germans could be defeated and that the Russians would probably return to the towns they had formerly occupied. As a result, these Poles and Ukrainians were more willing than they had previously been to help the beleaguered and threatened Jews. This was no consolation for the Jews, however, for word spread that the Germans, eager to complete the total annihilation of the Jews, were speeding up their plans to round them up and transport them to extermination camps. Understandably, the Jews were desperate.

Roald's father knew he had to act quickly. It was easy, at that time, to find a hiding place if enough money was available to pay for it, just as it was possible to buy one's way out of a labor camp. Fortunately, Hillel could pay for both with gold.

In early 1943, he arranged for his wife and son and two other members of the family to go into hiding. He remained behind, while they made their way to the home of a schoolteacher he had befriended, some twenty-five miles from the town. When Roald took refuge in that house, he was five and a half years old. When he left there, in June 1944, he was seven. In those fifteen months, he never left his hiding place:

'll tell you about the place we were hiding: *A village of about two hundred people. One brick house, the schoolhouse. The others were cottages, wooden cottages. The population was entirely Ukrainian: no Poles, no Jews. The schoolteacher was the only educated man in the town. He had a wife and two children. The wife didn't like the arrangement, but wives didn't speak against their husbands. They were an educated family. She respected her husband. They had two children. The children were about my age; one was older. Three rooms and a one-room schoolhouse on the first floor. The second floor was the school bath, and there was an attic, a regular attic. A very steep gable, and then there was a false attic, which was the last space above the real attic. And that's where we were, in the false attic. It was a long space, very, very steep. You could stand up only in the middle part of this false attic. You couldn't stand up in most of it. There was light only at the two ends. At one end,*

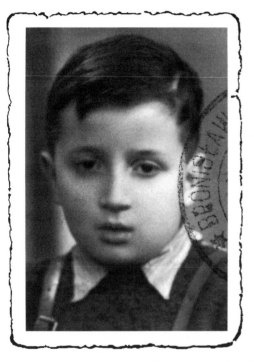

Roald Hoffmann
in 1944.

there was a brick taken out of the wall. At the other end, there were shutters, no glass, just shutters, closed, just for air to come in, to air out the space. Through the shutters, you could look down, and through the shutters or the brick, I could see the children playing outside.

The man would bring up food once a day and take away a pail of slops. We ate a lot of cabbage. This was rural Poland, Russia, in the winter. There were only the things that you put down in the store-house and underground cellar. At a certain point in the winter, you were down to potatoes, cabbages, and onions, apples and carrots—beets if you were lucky. The beets were done up differently, and they were preserved. All I remember is a lot of cabbage. I remember, too, sleeping on a pillow that was full of dried peas. That's what we used to put in our pillows. They make very comfortable pillows. We slept on some sort of thin, cotton mattress.

Roald, his mother, and his aunt and uncle were not allowed to leave the attic. There was a trap door that could be used—but only in case of fire. The days were long, and Roald is grateful to his mother for making the time pass usefully:

The real miracle was my mother keeping me quiet. A five-to-seven-year-old in that space. This was a schoolteacher, so there were some books and an atlas. My mother and I played a game where she would ask me, say, how would you get from Poland to San Francisco. It was not enough just to say, Well, you go that way—I had to tell her every mode of transportation from Zloczow. First we'd hail a peasant and take a cart ride, and then we'd get on a train and go to Lwow, and then we'd take another train, and then we'd get on a boat, and I'd have to name every place that we'd pass on the boat, and I would see how we would go. I know my geography very well. There were a few books. She taught me how to read. She taught me some math. She had some training as a schoolteacher. But I remember all the time being told to be quiet, the Germans will get you. . . .

Looking back on it now, months or years spent in a barn or in an attic would have seemed a luxury to Zelda Polofsky. Though a hiding place usually provided some kind of protection for a hidden child, during most of the three years she spent in hiding, Zelda had no such protection. For long periods of time, she lived in the woods.

Zelda, now a schoolteacher who lives near New York City, thinks she was born in 1932. She knows that she grew up in a small village near Vilna, Lithuania. At the time of her birth, Lithuania was under Polish rule, but following the German invasion of Poland in 1939, it was divided, and Vilna was occupied by the Russians, then Germany's allies. Though severe restrictions were enforced against the Jews, life was bearable for Zelda's family. Her father dealt in leather goods, and theirs was among the wealthiest families in the village. They were able to pay off the Russians and thereby avoided being sent to forced labor camps.

In the summer of 1941, the Nazis, having broken off their alliance with the Russians, invaded the Soviet Union. Shortly afterwards, they occupied Vilna and the towns surrounding it. Zelda herself was part of a naive group of Jews who warmly welcomed the German soldiers. One of those soldiers responded by shooting into the group at random, killing a man who was standing next to Zelda. This was the Nazis' way of making it clear that they were the masters.

The situation deteriorated rapidly for the Jewish population, which, forced to crowd into ghettos, awaited the inevitable roundups. The situation was hopeless, and it was Zelda who

Zelda Polofsky (on the left) and her older sister in Droysk, Poland, before the war.

alerted her family to the urgent need to go into hiding. She had been ill and confined to her bed:

After seven days of lying in bed, I was determined to get out. I got up very, very early. The ghetto was surrounded by a lake and the entrance to the ghetto was on just one side, so the Germans really didn't have to put out anybody to watch. So, I got up at seven o'clock or six o'clock, as soon as it got light—I couldn't wait to get out. We lived off a courtyard in one of the buildings, and behind the building was the lake. I went out to the lake, and I saw a policeman with a gun. And I knew that he was not supposed to be there. So I went back, and I woke up my mother, and I said, Something doesn't feel right. She came out and she saw it. She went back and she woke up my father. And those few minutes gave us enough time to run for our hiding place. We already heard stabbing and shooting around the town. See, they were coming from the outside into town, so that gave us enough time to run to the hiding place.

She recalls that hiding place, the way it had been prepared by her father, and their frantic efforts to reach it. Her memories of this episode that took place when she was a child are confusing, but her account conveys the panic and chaos felt by these people.

It was a building standing on big stones. There was no basement. So my father and some other man would pull out a stone every morning before they would go to work, and they would take out the dirt from the bottom. Every night, they would work there and then go to work in the morning. And then put back the stone in the morning. But then they had trouble with the dirt. What do you do with dirt? So they made like beds in a garden. At the same time that we started running toward that hiding place, men got on the rooftops in the courtyard and they started shooting. They were not Germans, they were people hired by the Germans, most of them, I didn't see any Germans at that point. I saw mainly people just shooting at us. People were running all over. They were trying to save themselves. We managed to get the stone out and to run into the hiding place. There was some food and water prepared. But people saw we were running, so they ran after us. There were a lot of people running with small children, and when my father saw that they were coming, that it was getting close, he just put in the stone, and he was on the outside. Now up on the roof was a man who recognized my father. He must have come from my town somewhere, from the villages, and he said, Michael, you run to the left and I'll shoot to the right. And then my father ran into the hiding place. I saw everything. I saw people running, we must have faced the water. People were running into the water, some dragging their children, some holding their children. You never know, we can say that we'll do this and we'll do that for our children, but when a time like this comes, you can't judge anybody. Some threw the children away, thinking that maybe they'd save themselves, but some just went in with their children. And there we were in our hiding place, and the shooting stopped slowly.

Once concealed under the building, they struggled to survive as the Germans tried to force them to surrender:

At night the men would go out. Most of the ghetto was all gone. The empty, empty homes were there, and food was there, and pil-

lows, and all kinds of things. They would bring these things into our hiding place. And there were big signs all over town saying that we know that some of you are hiding. See, they knew we couldn't go anywhere, and they knew, I guess, how many people there were, and the Germans must have realized. So they put out signs saying, Come out and you'll work and you'll be safe and whatever happened, happened. We stayed in, hoping that when we'd have a chance to get out, we'd get out. But we were afraid, because we figured they still must have surrounded the ghetto.

After five days they were discovered and captured and taken to a nearby building, where they were herded together with other Jews. Once again, Zelda's father managed to engineer an escape. Bribing a guard, he led a group of ten men, women, and children away from the ghetto. They walked more than twelve miles, along the back roads, to the home of Benetka, a farmer Zelda's father had once befriended. The farmer took them in and offered them his attic—in spite of the great risk to his own life and that of his daughter and grandchild with whom he lived. There was not nearly enough food for such a large group, however, and soon the farmer was forced to ask them to leave. Before they left, he offered refuge to Zelda and her family in case of emergency.

The group moved on. Their next stop was at the home of another farmer, where, to escape capture, they slept under stacks of hay in his barn. Unfortunately, their stay there was also a short one. Rumors of the presence of these refugees spread among the townspeople, and they had to move on.

Once again, Zelda's family resumed their wanderings in the woods. On one occasion, the young girl disobeyed her father—and it almost cost her her life.

My father told me I had to stay next to them. But I, I had to see everything around me. And in the woods, when you move away, all trees look alike. So I moved away from my father and, I don't know, I started walking, and all of a sudden I turned around and I just didn't see anybody. There I was, alone. So what do I do? I didn't know how to get out to find people. I must have been about nine and a half or ten, and I was wondering, What is going to happen to me now? And what should I do? I was trying to listen for some voices, because I knew I had to get out of the woods; I hadn't got a chance for survival there. And I started scraping up myself—to get out. Even to be shot, I had to be shot by somebody. I didn't want to die in there. So, I heard some noises and I started going toward those noises, and what do you think, it was my mother and father. I never told them I got lost, because I would have gotten it from my father.

Zelda is unable to forget the years she and her family spent desperately trying to survive in the woods. She remembers that Benetka would bring food to them whenever he could:

Through the years there were times that I almost died. I couldn't eat the food he gave us. Food—once a day, he used to have bread, and he would go to the pigs, clean out the pigs' place and then bring us, with his dirty hands, the piece of bread. I remember that when I would look at the dirt, I couldn't eat. There was very little food, very little, and even then I couldn't eat. I swelled up. People say that when a person swells up, they suffer from hunger. I didn't suffer from hunger. After a while I didn't want to eat. And my biggest problem, I mean, not mine but my parents', was where were they going to bury me? Because that was a big problem. One of the men

who was with us then said, We must do something. So he and my
father went and they got some food. My father knew other farmers.
They begged. At night, they took whatever food they were able to
pick from the fields. Carrots or potatoes. And I started coming back.
I remember—many times I think about it—whatever food there was,
was given to me. My mother, whatever food she had—maybe it
would have kept her alive—she gave it to me. And I took it, never
questioning. Many times I think about it.

Zelda thinks of the last months of her mother's life, following their forced departure from the house of another farmer:

We had no place to go. It was about Passover time. We were cross-
ing a lake, because you couldn't go on any roads. We were crossing
a lake and it was quite cold, and the ice broke and we all fell in. We
didn't drown, but there we were, wet, wintertime and no place to go.
We had a blanket. We must have had two blankets. We carried
whatever we had with us. I remember my father going into the
woods, and we were walking. Did you ever hang up something wet
in the wintertime? It becomes like a zombie. My father cleaned off
the snow and he put down the branches. He put the blanket on the
branches, and we lay down, all four of us, and we covered ourselves.
From our own breath, we became a little warmer. At that point, my
mother caught a cold. During the summertime, we would go in the
woods. We were hiding in the woods. There was one lady who knew
where we were, and she would bring us some food every night. And
I remember that if we had to travel during the summer that my
mother was sick, my father would pick her up, carry her, put her
down, bring the bundles, whatever we could carry, my sister and I,
and move on.

Weary and desperate, the family returned to the farmer's home:

He had a house, like a barn, for hay. Before he put the hay in, he put in a structure, and we would climb through the hay on our knees, all the way to the structure, unable to see there. And that is when my mother died. It was very bad. The man couldn't give us too much food. He didn't have enough for himself. But there was one man, a farmer, who lived very close to a town. He couldn't hide us, but he was very kind. And he had a lot of our goods, leather and stuff. This man held them for us. We would go there at night, and my father would pick up a piece of leather or whatever, and bring it to Benetka, and he would sell it, and this is how he was able to buy food. Everything had to be so careful, because, Why do you need so much food? Where did you get the leather? My father decided to go out at night and look for food to buy. Sometimes he would go into the fields and get something. And I remember, if he didn't come back in time, during the day he couldn't come into the hiding place. It would have to be at night only. And my mother must have been extremely sick—it was just before she was dying, but she couldn't die because her husband wasn't there. All night long, she kept on calling him, and she couldn't leave us. So in the morning, early in the morning, she heard my father starting to climb on his knees into the hiding place. And I remember she said, You're here. Now I can die. And she died. She died in the morning, and it was a very small place. I was afraid of her because she changed. After a while, during the day, her body swelled up, and I remember crawling into the furthest corner in that little hiding place until nighttime, when my father took her out, and we buried her.

FIVE

Hidden children are unanimous in believing that the Nazis robbed them of their childhoods. These young people, most of whom lived among strangers in unfamiliar surroundings, found it difficult to trust their hosts. They were always on their guard, always afraid that they might be discovered and captured. Most didn't know why—the youngest of them found it impossible to understand—yet they knew that their lives were in danger. They could rarely, if ever, relax.

There were, of course, many close calls. Zelda Polofsky remembers one. She and her parents were hiding under haystacks in the barn of a farmer who had offered them temporary refuge:

I remember a man from the village came to look for us, because, you see, my father used to snore. It was a terrible thing. One of my cousins, who was with us, complained because it kept him awake.

But it was a terrible thing, because, can you imagine, you go by a barn, around hay, and all of a sudden, there is a stack of hay and snoring is coming out of it? Somebody must have told on us. Because this man, this other farmer, he was a very nice man. He took us in. The villagers came; they were looking for Jews on the farms. For every Jew they found, they got a reward. I don't know, a bag of potatoes and some salt. So they came to this farm, and they came with pitchforks. They were going to find the Jews on that farm. And the farmer said to them, Why are you rushing? If I had Jews in my farm, where would they go? Come into the house. And he gave them whiskey and he gave them food, and as soon as it got dark, we took off.

Rosette Goldstein, hiding in the farmhouse in the French countryside, described another close call:

One day they came to the farm, and I happened to be the first one to see them. This time it was soldiers with rifles. They quickly put me in the bedroom underneath the mattress, between the spring and the mattress. The soldiers had come for food, because when they used to come around farmhouses, they knew they would get fresh food, and, they didn't care, they grabbed everything. This farm happened to have chickens, and that's what they came for. And I can remember, I don't know how, I don't know why I did it, I somehow got out and looked through the keyhole of the door. We had in the other room something like a chimney, because at that time everything was cooked on the open hearth, and they were standing in front of it with the guns. I can see it in front of me, these Nazis standing in front of the chimney. And I was lucky again—they left after they got their food. Had they found me, they probably would have shot everybody.

Sometimes these hidden children forgot their fears and disobeyed the orders of their elders. By doing so, they often endangered their own lives and the lives of their families. Klemak Nowicki was left alone each day while his mother went to work. He had been warned to keep to himself and to go out and play as little as possible, but sometimes the temptation to enjoy himself was too great:

I saw kids playing soccer, kicking the ball around, so I did go out. On one of these occasions, the landlady, not the owner but the landlady, cornered me against the building—I must have been between five and six—and I remember her being a large, kind of buxom person. All the kids suddenly stopped playing soccer, because she had cornered me and she asked me to pull my pants down, which, unfortunately, I did. I knew what she wanted to see. I felt utterly humiliated. And then she looked at my penis and saw that I was circumcised. Luckily, she did not call the Gestapo then. She waited for my mother to return from work. My mother did not look Jewish. She looked very Christian and, of course, she spoke Polish fluently and she was smart. Upon my mother's return, the landlady said to my mother, apologetically, I don't mean to insult you, but you know, I think your son is a Jew. My mother was very quick on her feet and said, Well, he's really adopted. I'm not sure, he may be a Jew, but he's adopted. He's not my son—to cover herself, you know. The landlady was satisfied, apparently, but my mother felt frightened. That night at midnight, we left the apartment building and went to a Catholic church, which someone told my mother was friendly to the Jews.

On two occasions, Stefanie Seltzer, a spirited four-year-old, endangered her life and that of her mother simply by talking too much. The first time this happened she was living in the Polish countryside without her mother. Though warned repeatedly of the possible consequences, she made a reference to her past, which revealed her identity as a Jew. As a result of this indiscretion, she was immediately returned to her mother in Warsaw.

She also spoke too much on another occasion, when she inadvertently called attention to the name changes that had become essential to their survival:

W e had just changed names, and I had another name. When the postman came and asked for my mother—I remember this very clearly—I was outside, and I said, That's what my mother's name used to be. Well, today it wouldn't matter, right? But it was very important then, and we had to leave. The woman we were staying with overheard me. Maybe the postman wouldn't have given me away. Those were guessing games: maybe the postman would have given me away, and maybe he wouldn't have. But, because nobody knew how this postman would react, we had to leave.

Stefanie Seltzer's behavior was perfectly normal for a small child; no four-year-old should be expected to deceive convincingly. But many of the hidden children, somewhat older than Stefanie, displayed remarkable maturity in handling life-threatening situations. They acted with ingenuity and with intelligence.

By thinking quickly, Jack Goldstein saved himself and his brother:

My father was working in the factory and my mother was out, and the Germans cordoned off the street. They had a truck or two trucks on the end of each street, and they wouldn't allow any traffic on it. Then they would go from house to house and take the Jews. There was a Jewish denouncer by the name of Jack Levine, they called him Fat Jack, who used to go with the Germans and point out Jews, or point out where the Jews lived. When it was time to visit Rue de Sel, they came into our building. They had attack boots on, so you heard them coming up the steps—they were old wooden stairs—and with the butts of their rifles they were banging against the doors to make the people open them, and yelling, Raus, raus, out, out. There were people crying and children screaming—terrible screaming. They came into our apartment, and just my brother and I were there, and we were praying, and this Fat Jack came with them, and they told us to take some belongings, to take some clothes and food, and to go with them. I was either seven or eight years old. I remembered, I knew, that my father was working in this factory, and I knew he had some kind of papers that supposedly exempted him from being arrested because he was pretty well skilled at making hats, so I said, Wait a minute. All the important papers were in the oven, and I took out this particular paper and showed it. He looked at it, and showed it to somebody else, and they said, they didn't say anything, they gave it back to me and they left. They took all the people from the building. Then, at the end, they came back, and this Fat Jack said, What are we doing with these boys? This one guy looked at us and said, It appears in order, and the papers are all right. Nothing, leave them. So they left us. That was a close call.

Benno Horowitz also avoided being captured through quick thinking. Though hidden safely with his family in the French

Alps, he wanted to resume his studies in Lyon, in the south of France, where he had lived and studied before going into hiding. A teenager capable of making his own decisions, he traveled to Lyon, over his mother's objections, and rented a room from the French family that had befriended and rented rooms to the Horowitzes in the past. He remained there for only two days:

You have to understand, at that time nobody liked it when the doorbell or the phone rang. And at seven o'clock on the second night, the doorbell rang. It was the police looking for my father, and he wasn't there. When they asked if his son was there, the landlady said she knew nothing. But we took nothing lightly. When the bell had rung, I knew I had to get on my toes and go into hiding. It so happened that the apartment had a long hallway. We were in the kitchen, eating in the kitchen, at seven o'clock, and the door was closed. So on my tiptoes, I went to the other end of the hall; there was another door at the other end. Fortunately there were no police at the building door, and so I slipped out. I never went back, and I returned to the mountains.

Frequently children were saved by the courage and kindness of outsiders. While hiding in a convent, Klemak Nowicki's life was saved by a clergyman:

Occasionally, through neighbors, the Germans would get to know that the convent was hiding Jews. They would make surprise visits to arrest the Jewish kids. I remember one time I was playing in the sandbox outside. A nun came and grabbed me, and dragged me inside the building to hide me under a bed. The Gestapo searched the building for Jews. More girls than boys survived for obvious reasons. Because they were circumcised, it was easier to identify the Jewish boys than girls. That happened on a couple of occasions when the Gestapo came to search for Jews. On one occasion they caught me. I remember the scene when they were taking me out. About three men were taking me out, and I remember that the bishop, the retired bishop who lived on the grounds, came and intervened, and he said, If you take him, you'll have to take me. I don't know why, but they let me go. They usually didn't give a damn, they'd take everybody. But they left me alone. If it wasn't for the bishop's intervention, I would have been dead.

Edith Knoll had a close call when traveling with her father and her cousin. She saved her own life by understanding that even a German official was a human being:

My father and I and my cousin went on the train, and two railroad stations after Brussels we were arrested. There was a man in the same compartment, and somehow I had the feeling that he was watching us and something wasn't quite right. He was reading a paper, but I saw him look over the paper. I couldn't say anything— most of our conversations were with our eyes, and I looked at my father and he looked at me, and we knew things were not right, but we couldn't do anything. We were taken off the train, and this man said we were arrested and had to go back to Brussels. On the train back to Brussels, I said to one of the Germans, "Tell me, do you have children?" And he told me, "Yes. I have a son fighting in Russia." "Do you hear from him?" I asked. He said, "No, we haven't heard from him." And I told him, "That must be terrible for you and your wife." I think that this question, this approach to him, saved my life. I think this man really felt that—you know how you feel sometimes if you do something good—maybe I'll be rewarded and I'll see my son again. Because soon after that, he said to me, "I'm going to send you back to your mother." I said to him, "What about my father?" "He will be home in three days." The man was a righteous Christian. He rescued me. He let me out a side door, put me in a cab with my little cousin and a pregnant lady. Of course, my father never came back. I was given a second to say good-bye to him. A hug. Our eyes met. I was so petrified. It was incredible. I never saw him again. He was taken to prison in Brussels and then deported to Auschwitz. I still have the last letter he wrote to us.

One of the first and most difficult lessons hidden children had to learn was to remain silent. A cry or a laugh—the basic, familiar sounds of childhood—might reveal their presence to a mysterious enemy, an enemy ready to punish them for crimes they never committed. "I knew that it was a matter of life or death that I didn't cry and that I didn't fuss," Alice Sondike remembers. "I do know one thing, and that is that I never cried. I remember my own kids, and now I have grandchildren, and when their mother leaves the room, they get hysterical. But I never cried."

Rachelle Goldstein, only three and a half years old at the time, remembers not being allowed to cry after having been left in the office of the mother superior in a Belgian convent.

They left me alone with Mother Superior and another nun. There were two nuns. All of a sudden it hit me, What's going on here? I had been told I was going out for a day in the country. So I started to scream my head off. I started crying, I want my mother. Their way of dealing with it was to lock me in a closet, and they said, When you stop crying, you can come out. So there I was in the closet, scared out of my wits, a black, dark closet. It was light when I went in there, and it was dark when I came out, so I must have been in there a long time.

She also remembers being told that it was important to remain silent. She was too young to understand that the Germans might search the convent for hidden Jews.

They would take me and two other children, a boy and a girl, Paul and Claire, and they would drop us down in a coal chute into the coal cellar. We were told not to cry, not to breathe, and not to move, because we would die if we did. At that time I had no idea why. I didn't even realize that the other children didn't go through similar experiences. But one day, I remember I must have been six or so, it was way after the war, I shot up in bed suddenly thinking, Paul and Claire were Jewish. By then, of course, I realized I was Jewish. But it took that long for me to realize that those other kids must have been Jewish, too.

Stefanie Seltzer's rescuers did not allow her to express her feelings, even after she heard a devastating piece of news:

Even when I was told that much of my family had been killed, I was not allowed to cry or make any noise, because that annoyed them. I remember the night that I was told that the people in my family had been killed. I went to bed and cried, and I was scolded and beaten, and told not to make any noise. I ripped my nails out—I got into my cuticles and ripped them off, I guess in an attempt to squelch the noise coming out. And I remember that the tips of my fingers were absolutely bloody and pulpy, messy from being so tight and trying to contain everything.

Klemak Nowicki learned the importance of silence while traveling by train to the convent where he was to be hidden:

I remember that ride, because my mother would always carefully instruct me on how I should behave. I was very curious. I would look around and talk to strangers. She told me not to talk, not to look around, to look down at my feet, etc. And she covered my face with a shawl to hide me as much as possible. And I remember her kicking my feet whenever I started to look around or talk to somebody. So I was already taught to be quiet and to hide.

Edith Knoll learned the importance of remaining silent while being smuggled out of Germany into Belgium:

I was handed over to a stranger—a lady who took me by trolley car or tram over the border. She had a child of her own of my age, but she didn't have a picture of this child in her passport, only her name and the dates. I had to remain silent. I had a big scarf put around my head. Only my eyes were not covered, and I was told not to say anything, since I didn't speak the language and I was supposed to be Belgian. She maintained that I had had a tonsillectomy, and this is how I got over the border. I cannot tell you how scary this was. You just stop breathing at times. . . .

Zelda Polofsky witnessed a tragic event while hidden with fifty other Jews under an abandoned building in Warsaw:

HOWARD

GREENFELD

Some of the people came in with young children, and there was no way to keep them quiet. There was one child, he must have been eighteen months old, and he kept on crying and crying. The father tried to choke him, but he couldn't. So, everybody else in the hiding place tried to choke the child, because we'd have been discovered, and there must have been about fifty people—there was so much death surrounding us—and my father and this other man just couldn't choke the child. They said, If we'll be discovered, we'll be discovered. At this point the father said, I cannot have fifty people sacrificed for my child, and he killed him. And I remember thinking that I wanted him dead, too, because I knew if he didn't die, we'd be all discovered.

PART THREE

LIBERATION

It was an incredible feeling to be outside and not to worry anymore, but it took me a couple of months to walk normally. I was so scared of footsteps, and so afraid that something could happen, because we had always been in such danger, and it was always a question of life or death. But I had received the gift of life. . . .

—Edith Knoll

SIX

On June 6, 1944, Allied forces invaded continental Europe, landing on the coast of Normandy, France. That day, which became known as D-Day, marked the beginning of the end of the German occupation of Western Europe. On August 23, Paris was liberated, and on September 4, Brussels was freed from Nazi rule.

Over the next several months, Soviet troops swept through Eastern Europe, making the Allied victory complete. During this period, too, the death camps were opened by American, British, and Soviet forces, and the few prisoners who had miraculously managed to survive the Nazi atrocities were set free. On April 30, 1945, Adolf Hitler committed suicide in Berlin, and on May 7, Germany surrendered unconditionally to the Allies.

The Holocaust had come to an end. Hitler had not fully realized his dream of annihilating the Jewish people, but he had come close to achieving it. With the defeat of the Nazis, those children who had remained hidden during the war could finally come out into the open and reclaim their identity. Yet their liberation was not always an easy one. After years of darkness, they had difficulty adjusting to the light of freedom, and most struggled to find their way.

For some children, the struggle began immediately following liberation. Alice Sondike was one of these. Very young when she went into hiding, the initial readjustment to life with her parents was painful. Both parents had survived concentration camps. Her father had been in Dachau, the first of the camps within Germany, and her mother had been in Auschwitz, where two million people had died. Her mother was the first to find her, in the home of the German couple who had wanted to adopt her. She had learned of Alice's whereabouts by carefully tracing her moves from the time they had separated. At first, the couple refused to give her up. They hid the young girl in a closet, hoping that her mother would go away without her. But when they were told that they had been giving shelter to a *Jewish* child, they were horrified and changed their minds. They literally threw her out the door. "As much of a shock as it was to them, you can't believe what a shock it was to me," Alice remembers today.

She had difficulty adjusting to life with her parents. They were strangers to her, merely one more couple with whom she was to live, and, too young to understand their pain, she treated them badly:

Alice Sondike in a refugee camp in Germany.

So here was a fourth couple. My mother was in such bad shape, both physically and emotionally. I could never understand, of course, being a child. But she had no teeth. She was a young woman, and she had no teeth. She was, I mean, terrible! And I said it to her. I couldn't stand being near her. You know how children can be. After all these years of being on my own and learning how to manipulate people, boy, did I manipulate her: I hate you. You're disgusting. Get me this, buy me that. She was like putty in my hands. Then my father came back. He had been in Dachau and he was liberated by the Americans. He had been sick. He had typhus, so he had been in the hospital for a while. I remember the day he came. I remember I was walking with my mother in the street. She was carrying things and I was walking next to her. We went to this place where, you know, the survivors were registering, and someone said to her, Oh, does your husband have curly blond hair and has he glasses? A man came, and it was him! We were quite an oddity among the survivors, because we were a family that was intact. It was a rarity that a mother, a father, and a child survived. I mean, people would point at us in the street. You know, those are the ones! They would point at us because it was such an oddity.

Most children, however, experienced a period of joy and euphoria before their struggles began. One of them, Rachelle Goldstein, looked forward eagerly to her parents' arrival. She was an infant when she had gone into hiding and was at first unable to recognize them:

Once I knew the war was over, I just went around every waking moment saying, My parents are coming, my parents are coming.

I remember I was in the garden, we were making these hats out of newspaper—What do you call them? they're a boat one way, and a hat the other—and I had this thing on my head, and somebody came over and said, There is someone here to see you. And I just tossed it off my head, I remember doing that, and saying, My parents are here. I ran over to the mother superior's office and ran in there, and I saw a man and a woman. I did not recognize them at all and the woman just grabbed me. And once she grabbed me, I knew, That's my mother.

Gisele Warshawsky was in a small town in the Ardennes, very near the fighting that raged during the last months of the war, when, after a long wait, she was reunited with her mother:

Then it happened. The church bells rang out. Victory was on our side. A lot of activity was going on at the Institut. We had seen soldiers and men from the resistance coming and going, but we were told to say nothing. Our counselors left many nights and returned by morning. We realized that they, too, worked for the Belgian resistance. We realized how close we had been during the fighting. We ran out into the street, which was lined by the populace of the small town. Everyone was shouting with excitement as the Americans marched through the street. We were shouting what one of the sisters had told us to shout in English: "Thank you!" What a thrill it was to see the Americans and Belgian resistance fighters marching through!

That spring of 1945, many Belgian parents picked up their children. Others began to leave, until only the Jewish girls remained.

We deliberated between us how many had a parent or parents still alive. I knew my mother had been hidden—how would she find me now? Anxiety began to creep into all our hearts. We acted happy on the outside, but now that everything was in the open, everyone would find out we were Jewish—fear began to show its ugly face.

Rumors seeped through: the Germans were going to begin one last attack. The war was not yet over for us. Shortly after, we were told to pack our belongings. It was no longer safe for us to remain at the Institut. We left during the night on two army trucks and departed this wonderful haven. I had been there for one and one-half years. We traveled all night and slept fitfully on the truck. By morning, we arrived at the outskirts of Brussels and we were placed in another Catholic orphanage.

Gisele and her mother at home in Brussels in 1946.

I stayed there with my group for two weeks, hoping to hear from my mother. One day, the mother superior called me into her parlor—I had two visitors. I ran into the waiting arms of my darling mother, hugging, kissing, and crying. There was also Mrs. De Rudder, who had come along to make sure Mother was all right and to find me. Of course, I wanted to leave immediately. I could speak only in French and recalled little German or Flemish, although I still understood both. Mother spoke Flemish to me; I could not answer. Mrs. De Rudder was our translator. All I could still say was, "Mama, veine nicht!"—Mama, don't cry! These were *tears of joy at seeing me again—I was skinny perhaps, but safe and sound.*

Klemak Nowicki, whose father had died in a concentration camp, waited for his mother in the basement of the convent in which he was hidden. He was afraid he would not live to see her again. It was a fear shared by many of these children.

The way the war ended for us, the Allies—I guess it must have been the Russians—thought that there were Germans hidden in this convent. So they were attacking us. Actually, there was cannon fire on the building. I was hiding in the basement, and I remember that there was a direct hit on the window. The nuns, luckily, had blocked the window with bricks. There was a direct hit near the window, and I remember seeing red and being thrown against the wall, hearing this big boom. It was terrifying. The nuns went out with a white flag or something, I think, after that. We couldn't eat. For a long time, all we had was water and kind of half-cooked noodles. When we put the flag out, the white flag, I remember they came in with guns drawn, inspecting everything, searching for Germans in the convent. So that's how I was liberated. Then we all waited for our parents to return to pick us up. Many never returned. Those were the most dramatic and touching scenes of my childhood. Waiting for my mother to come back . . .*

His joy when his mother finally arrived was boundless:

Every time someone would come to the front door, all the kids would run up there and think it was their parents, and, of course all

of them, except one, would be disappointed. That was the most dif-
ficult moment for us. Waiting. Repeated disappointments. One of
these times, my mother did in fact come. She had been evacuated
herself. The Germans had evacuated people outside of Warsaw. So
she returned, walking a hundred miles, riding in horse carts, what-
ever moved, just to pick me up. That's how my liberation occurred,
and that's how my hiding ended, the physical hiding. It was a big
moment.

Jack Goldstein's moment came in June 1944, before the end of
the war. Following the Normandy landing, the area surrounding
the convent in which he was hidden was subjected to nightly
bombing attacks. Most of the inhabitants of the convent were
moved to a common shelter, but Jack, sick and with a high fever,
was placed in an attic by himself. Somehow, his mother sensed
that her son was not well, and, risking her life, she made her way
to the convent. Her arrival there was the fulfillment of his dream:

I still remember that there was a bombing, and I was lying there in
my bed, and I saw this apparition—my mother was a very attrac-
tive person—and I thought it was like an angel, and it was my
mother walking into the room. And she saw how sick I was. This was
very close to the liberation of Brussels—I think maybe it was about
two weeks before the liberation—and she decided that she was going
to take my brother and me out of this home. And she did, and she
took us back to Brussels.

The news from the war front looked better every day. We were get-
ting closer and closer. There was a store downstairs, and I don't
know how they did it, but they had started manufacturing flags. At

first they said the Russians were coming to liberate us, so we went downstairs and bought Russian flags. Then, they said the English were coming, so we went running down to get English flags. Then, they said the Americans were coming, and finally the ones that did come were Americans. I think it was late August, early September. The Allies came in with tanks and trucks, and they threw chocolate to the kids, and chewing gum.

Rosette Goldstein recalls only the thrill and the excitement of liberation. Her mother came to get her in 1945, having walked part of the way from Paris because the trains had been derailed. Before returning to the French capital, the mother and daughter spent a few days at the farm where Rosette had been hidden. They watched the American convoys pass by, and they ran to the road to bring them fruits and vegetables. In return, the soldiers gave them chocolate bars, candy that symbolized their return to the childhood they had lost.

Frank Siegel also has joyful memories of the arrival of the American soldiers. Shortly after the liberation of Belgium, his father had come to Ciney to bring him home. On the way home, they watched the Americans pass by.

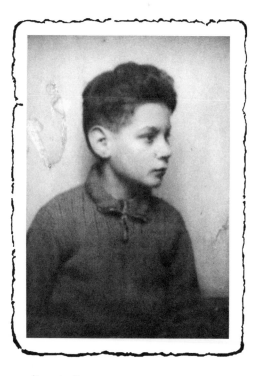

Frank Siegel

I remember them throwing flowers, and one guy had his mouth open, and he threw them in the mouth of an officer, you know, what a lucky shot. They threw us chewing gum. And we were eating this chewing gum, and we were saying to each other, What kind of crazy food is it that you chew and you don't swallow? We swallowed, and I guess it's okay, I'm still alive.

Benno Horowitz and Edith Knoll vividly remember the exhilaration they felt. Benno learned the end of the war was at hand following the landing of the Allies at Normandy. He was exuberant: "Nothing could duplicate such an exciting day. It meant our freedom, surviving, living, the right to live."
And Edith remembers the jubilance that accompanied the liberation of Belgium: "You can't describe that feeling. People were dancing in the street. The nuns were dancing in the street, and the nuns were kissing the soldiers, and everyone was hugging everybody. It was like an explosion."

Benno Horowitz listened to broadcasts from Switzerland and London on his "instrument of survival." A photograph of Winston Churchill sits on top of the radio.

Inevitably, the time of flowers and chocolates and hugging and dancing came to an end. Once out of hiding, these children had to face a world far different from the one they had known. They had lost many—or even most—members of their families. Most were homeless and even stateless, their possessions plundered and their roots severed. Upon returning to their cities and villages, many were greeted with hostility by former neighbors who, in their ignorance and blind hatred of Jews, blamed them for the war. Roald Hoffmann, Fran Greene, and Zelda Polofsky were among those.

When Roald Hoffmann and his mother left their attic hiding place for the first time in fifteen months, they walked across muddy fields to the Russian lines. From there, they were taken by truck to the town where they had lived, which was under Russian control. The return was disheartening. They were alone, Roald's father having been shot in a public execution. There was nothing left for them in their town. They were received with suspicion instead of compassion by people who assumed and probably hoped they had been killed. They stayed there, unwelcome, for only a few months, moving afterward from town to town, until they were placed in a refugee camp.

Fran Greene's fate was even more painful. Frozen and hungry when she and her parents were liberated by the Russians, she returned with them to the barn where they had hidden. There they found the bodies of Fran's grandparents and little brother, together with remnants of their clothing. They buried them and left. When they returned to their hometown, they found that their house had been destroyed. Afraid that their Polish neighbors, who held them responsible for the war, would kill them, they lived in the basement of another house, fed and protected by the Russians. Their fears were justified. On one of his visits to the site of their hiding place, Fran's father was shot and killed by irate Polish citizens. It was six months after the war had ended.

Zelda Polofsky and her father, too, were near exhaustion when they were liberated by the Rus-

Roald Hoffmann and his mother in Krakow in 1945.

sian army. Unable to walk at first, her father thought about suicide, but was sustained by his need to tell the world what had happened to the Jewish people. They returned to their town to find that only about 27 of the 550 Jewish inhabitants had survived. Unwanted in their own country, they began another long and painful journey, which ended in the United States.

Zelda's health card issued on April 6, 1949, in a refugee camp in Germany.

AJDC-CC-OSE MEDICAL DEPARTMENT

Health Card № 104534

(N)

Issued only to persons who were found free from disease or have been successfully treated.

Name: CYPUK ZELDA

Sex: F 15 XII 35.

FOR MEDICAL PURPOSES ONLY.

Signature

SEVEN

Following the years of silence and fear, most of the hidden children wandered throughout Europe in search of new homes and new lives. For many of them, the first stop was one of the displaced persons' camps set up to provide temporary housing for these refugees. They then moved to whatever country would accept them. Some were unable to face the new traumas that awaited them—in most cases, having to rebuild families and start life all over again. They suffered psychiatric illnesses, and some committed suicide. They had been emotionally damaged during the war and were unable to recover. Maya Freed, who spent the war in a series of foster homes and orphanages, is today a psychotherapist. She remembers always feeling like a battered child, though she was never physically abused. "The worst kind of abuse a child can experience," she believes, "is neglect. Physical abuse and sexual abuse are awful. But emotional neglect is the closest you can come to the death of a child, because if there's no sense of self, there can be no sense of security."

Many others were able to survive once again and to remake their lives; of these, a large number left Europe and settled in Israel or the United States.

Only recently have these men and women started to talk of their Holocaust experiences. For more than forty years they remained silent—remained, it can be said, in hiding, unable to share this period of their lives with their families or friends.

They felt that their stories were insignificant compared with the horrible stories of the Nazi concentration camps and they were told repeatedly that they should forget the past, that they should consider themselves lucky to have survived, that talking about it would only make matters worse. Gisele Warshawsky suffered what is known as survivor's guilt. She wonders why she had lived while those she loved had died: "The Germans had done terrible things to us as a family. I lost three years of my childhood, in addition to my loss of identity. But I suffered more from the loss of my beloved brother and sister. Why am I here, and not them?" Most often, these hidden children were told that they were too young to have really suffered: adult survivors had most deeply felt the pain, and they were the ones who needed help and compassion. In the light of these attitudes, most of the hidden children preferred to remain silent.

Rosette Goldstein expressed it in this way:

Nobody wanted to listen to us. They all said, You were very lucky, and that's it. Don't talk about it anymore. But I always knew I was different, and whenever we [hidden children] meet, what draws us to-

gether is the feeling that we are very different from other people. We always felt that way, but people didn't want to listen to us. . . .

I never thought I was a Holocaust survivor. I went to a meeting in the city, and they asked Holocaust survivors to stand up. What am I? Am I a survivor, or am I second-generation? I'm not second-generation, I'm a survivor. People are saying to us, Forget it, that's it, finished. They didn't realize the hurt, the loneliness.

In the spring of 1991, the First International Gathering of Children Hidden During World War II was held under the auspices of the Anti-Defamation League of B'nai B'rith in New York City. A month before the meeting, 350 hidden children had agreed to attend. By the time the conference opened, 1,600 had registered and 1,500 others had written to say that although they were unable to attend the New York conference, they wanted to participate in future gatherings.

Finally, the hidden children had found a voice. Now they were able to share their experiences with others who had suffered as they had and who could understand. They were eager to tell their stories, for they, the youngest survivors of Hitler's fury, knew they were the last witnesses. Rosette Goldstein told me:

We have to talk. We are the last ones. After us, there's nobody. And there are too many people out there who are trying to say that the Holocaust didn't happen. Isn't that something? That it didn't happen the way it did. That's why we have to talk, why you have to write. I mean, our kids have to know, not only our kids, but the whole world. And all types of children, not only Jewish children, it's got to be everybody. . . .

Bauer, Yehuda. *A History of the Holocaust*. New York: Franklin Watts, 1982.

Block, Gay, and Malka Drucker. *Rescuers: Portraits of Moral Courage in the Holocaust*. New York: Holmes & Meier, 1992.

Dawidowicz, Lucy S. *The War Against the Jews, 1933–1945*. New York: Holt, Rinehart and Winston, 1975.

Des Pres, Terrence. *The Survivor: An Anatomy of Life in the Death Camps*. New York: Oxford University Press, 1976.

Dwork, Debórah. *Children with a Star: Jewish Youth in Nazi Europe*. New Haven: Yale University Press, 1991.

Frank, Anne. *The Diary of Anne Frank: The Critical Edition*. New York: Doubleday, 1989.

Friedländer, Saul. *When Memory Comes*. New York: Farrar, Straus and Giroux, 1979.

Gilbert, Martin. *The Holocaust: A History of the Jews of Europe During the Second World War*. New York: Holt, Rinehart and Winston, 1985.

Hilberg, Raul. *Perpetrators Victims Bystanders: The Jewish Catastrophe 1933–1945*. New York: HarperCollins, 1992.

Johnson, Paul. *A History of the Jews*. New York: Harper & Row, 1987.

Lanzmann, Claude. *Shoah: An Oral History of the Holocaust*. New York: Pantheon, 1985.

Lewin, Rhoda G., ed. *Witness to the Holocaust: An Oral History*. New York: Macmillan, 1989.

Meltzer, Milton. *Never to Forget: The Jews of the Holocaust*. New York: Harper & Row, 1976.

Moskovitz, Sarah. *Love Despite Hate: Child Survivors of the Holocaust and Their Adult Lives*. New York: Schocken Books, 1983.

Rittner, Carol, and Sondra Myers, eds. *The Courage to Care: Rescuers of Jews During the Holocaust*. New York: New York University Press, 1986.

Tec, Nechama. *When Light Pierced the Darkness: Christian Rescue of Jews in Nazi-Occupied Poland*. New York: Oxford University Press, 1986.

Wiesel, Elie. *Night*. New York: Bantam, 1982.

Note: For an extraordinarily moving evocation of the Holocaust, I recommend the two volumes of *Maus*, by Art Spiegelman, published by Pantheon Books, New York, in 1986 and 1991. Using the form of a cartoon strip to recount the story of his father's survival during and after the Holocaust, Spiegelman makes a unique contribution to the literature of those years.

INDEX

Page numbers in italic type refer to photographs.

115